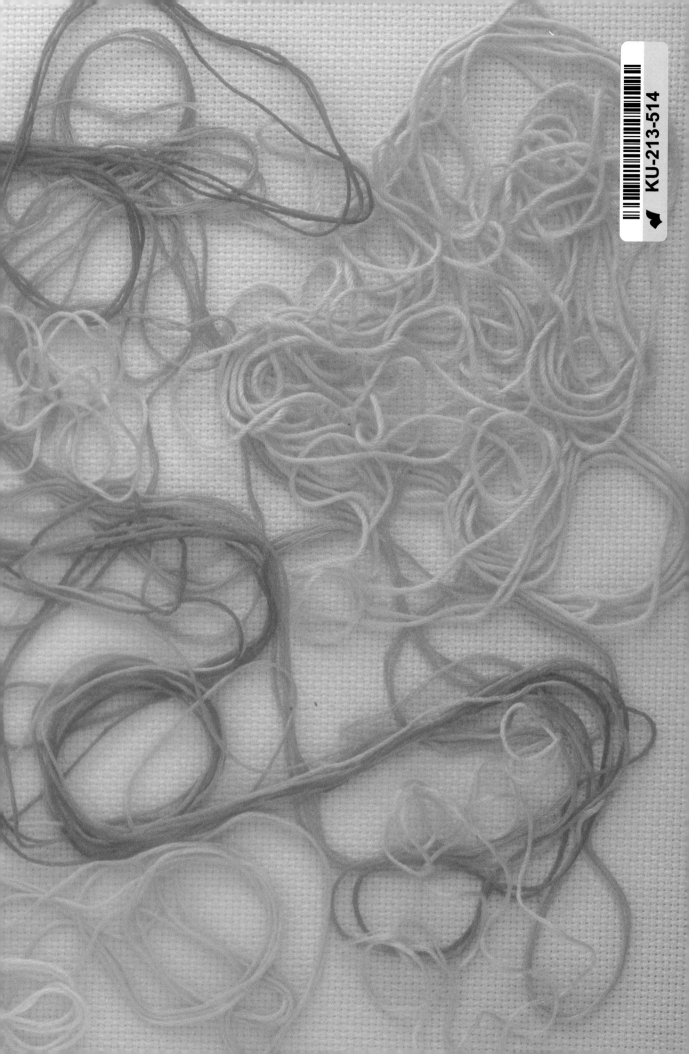

A PRACTICAL GUIDE TO
Cross-Stitch

Three images of the birth of Jesus Christ, stitched on linen fabric, mounted on board and ready to be hung at Christmas time.

This beautiful oblong cushion is stitched in Danish Flower thread.

A PRACTICAL GUIDE TO
Cross-Stitch

Jennifer Rollins

An example of an early European-style sampler.

This edition produced exclusively in the UK for WH Smith Ltd.
Greenbridge Road, Swindon SN3 3LD.

Published by Jigsaw Publishing
Suite 4, 214 Military Road, Neutral Bay NSW 2089

Publisher: Graham Fill
Editor: Lisa Foulis
Photographer: Andrew Elton
Designer: Susie Baxter Smith, Jan Smith
Illustrations: Jan Smith

First Published 1991
© Copyright: Jigsaw Publishing
© Copyright Design: Jigsaw Publishing

Typesetting: Accuset Phototypesetting Pty Ltd
Produced in Hong Kong by Mandarin

National Library of Australian Cataloguing-in-Publication
Data:

Rollins, Jennifer.
A Practical guide to cross stitch.

Includes index.
ISBN 1 875555 00 5

1. Cross-stitch — Patterns. I. Title.

746.443041

Contents

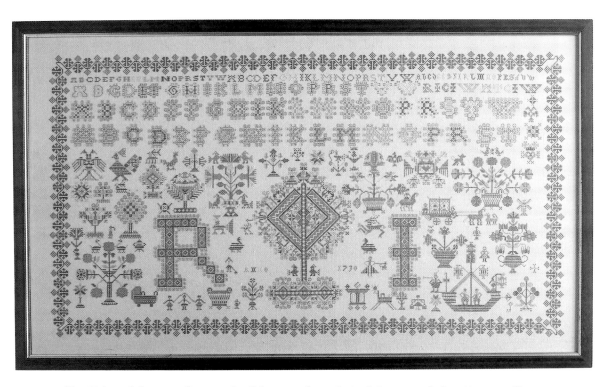

Traditional images feature in this sampler, stitched in stranded cotton on linen.

Introduction

Counted cross-stitch is a form of embroidery that has been practised for centuries by both men and women as an occupation and a leisure activity. This book contains an historical perspective on counted cross-stitch, plus practical information on the tools and material necessary to do the craft, and a comprehensive stitch guide.

Techniques on creating charts for your own designs, and how to mount and frame them are explained in easy-to-follow steps, accompanied by detailed illustrations.

A chapter on designing your own sampler contains valuable hints on how to combine traditional and modern motifs into a charming piece. Twenty projects, with detailed instructions and easy-to-follow charts, have been designed to take the stitcher through from simple to more complicated counted cross-stitch treasures.

The History of Cross-Stitch

A colourful sampler featuring images of trees, birds and the church.

The history of embroidery is almost as long as the history of civilisation itself; in fact, embroidery may qualify as one of the oldest of the decorative crafts. Primitive spinning and weaving were originally practised in around 10,000 BC. Evidence of the existence of woven cloth and the fact that it was joined together by thread comes from archaeological finds of coarse cloth, either woven or plaited, and bone and bronze needles dating from around 3000 to 2000 BC.

The earliest examples of decorative embroidery were found in Egyptian tombs dating from around 1000 BC, although most embroidery originated from tombs of the Coptic period which began in the first century AD. Cross-stitch is thought to have originated with the Copts, although the perishable nature of natural fabrics and the scarcity of samples from this period make it difficult to precisely determine the origin and spread of particular embroidery stitches. Indeed, the discovery of wall paintings and sculptures from much earlier periods suggest the use of embroidery as a decorative feature on clothing; however, no examples have survived.

The ancient Greeks were skilled at weaving flax, but while very few samples of their work remain, Homeric literature refers to the importance of embroidery amongst Greek women. The earliest scraps date from the fourth century BC and demonstrate the Greeks' facility with satin, knot and chain stitches. Similar examples from Scythian sites in southern Russia have also been found and testify to the trade links that existed between these two cultures.

Cross-stitch was used extensively from around 600 to 900 AD in China, India, Egypt, Greece and Rome, although due to the complex nature of trading and emigration patterns during this period, it is impossible to determine which culture influenced which in regard to embroidery techniques and designs.

England has a long tradition of stitching, with perhaps the most famous embroidery in the world, the Bayeux Tapestry, which originated from the workshop of a group of English craftsmen in the second half of the eleventh century. This tapestry, the original of which is in France, was commissioned by the Bishop of Bayeux for a new church.

The most important period in English embroidery history occurred in the mid-thirteenth to mid-fourteenth centuries when *opus anglicanum* (English work) was considered the finest in Europe. It was highly sought after as decoration for the robes of the clergy, and many surviving examples of this work are still to be found in the churches and museums of the major cities of Europe.

The fifteenth century saw a coarsening and stereotyping of designs, inferior workmanship, and an increasing reliance on Italian silk brocades and velvets to create the effect of opulence that had previously been achieved with embroidery. Also gaining popularity was the technique of embroidering motifs separately and then appliquéing them onto costly fabrics.

With the Reformation came the end of the great tradition of English ecclesiastical embroidery, although the *opus anglicanum* theme had been in decline well before then. Instead, an interest in domestic decoration, spurred on by the increased prosperity and settled conditions of the Tudor and Elizabethan periods, saw the rise of the amateur embroiderer, whose main concern was with the decoration of functional household items such as footstools, wall hangings and cushions.

Crossed stitches of various types were used extensively in embroideries of this period, usually in combination with other stitches such as tent stitch and satin stitch. Wools and silks were the preferred embroidery threads and the background fabric was usually linen. Embroidery samplers were also produced in great numbers and were designed to demonstrate a young woman's skill and range of stitches.

Jacobean wool work, later called crewel embroidery, was popular in the seventeenth century and was used to decorate bed curtains and other large hangings. Crewel wools were also taken to America by the early settlers but, unlike the Indian and Chinese motifs used by European embroiderers, American embroidery was dominated by floral designs. Colours were limited to those produced by vegetable dyes, with blue being the most predominant colour seen in early American embroidery. Only a few stitches were used, including cross-stitch, satin and herringbone stitches and French knots.

During the eighteenth century embroidery on cloth and furnishings was influenced by Chinese designs. France, too, rose to pre-eminence with its delicate silk embroideries.

Berlin wool work, which became popular in England and America in the nineteenth century and remained in vogue for half a century, used bright colours and sentimental motifs such as pets and bouquets of flowers for embroidered pictures designed to be displayed on walls. The early designs imported from Berlin used tent and cross-stitches worked in worsted wools. As its popularity grew, however, beads, jewels, pearls and sequins were added and Berlin wool work covered every conceivable household item.

With the advent of mass-produced, printed fabrics and a change in the style of interior decoration, embroidery started to decline in popularity in the 1870s. It was not until the 1920s that a revival took place. Initiated in Denmark, a fresh look at traditional techniques led to new designs for cross-stitch and drawn thread work. The opportunity for and ease of travelling also enabled women to examine embroidery from different cultures and to utilise the techniques they discovered in their own designs.

Modern cross-stitch need not be limited to traditional fabrics. Experimentation with colour, thread and fabric and with the vast range of other craft techniques available means that these days cross-stitch is only limited by your imagination. If you take the time to learn the traditional techniques that form the basis of the craft (since many of these techniques are still used even with the most avant-garde designs), then a completely new world of an ancient decorative craft will be open to you.

Choosing the Right Materials

*T*here are very few specific items needed to create a piece of cross-stitch apart from fabric, thread and needle. The choice of these, however, will determine the final appearance of your work. The projects in this book have been designed to be stitched on Aida, linen and even-weave fabrics, and are worked in stranded cotton. Following is an explanation of all of the types of fabric that you will become familiar as you progress from a beginner to an expert.

BACKGROUND FABRIC

The background fabric is the material upon which the cross-stitch design is worked, the choice of fabric depending on such things as the purpose for which the work is destined, the type of embroidery thread you wish to use and the fineness or detail of the design you have chosen. Obviously a cushion cover for the family room couch worked in wool thread will require a sturdier backing fabric than a delicate sampler using fine cotton thread intended for framing behind glass.

Generally speaking, there are three types of fabric used in cross-stitch: even-weave fabric, plain-weave fabric, and canvas.

Even-weave fabric

The most traditional even-weave fabric, that is, a fabric with the same number of horizontal and vertical threads, is linen (Fig. 1). The thread count (the number of warp and weft threads per square inch [per sq. cm.]) dictates the tightness or fineness of the weave and, therefore, the size of the stitch. There are various grades of linen available for cross-stitch from very coarse to very fine, and your choice will depend on the project you have in mind.

Fig. 1. Even-weave fabric

Even-weave fabrics especially designed for cross-stitch are also available, the most common of these being Aida fabric which is woven in blocks of four threads horizontally and vertically (Fig. 2). The basket-weave design of this fabric makes it much

Fig. 2. Even-weave Aida fabric

easier to embroider, as squares rather than individual linen threads are being counted. Aida fabric is available in counts of 11, 14, 16 stitches per inch. It is available in cream, plus a wide variety of colours for the more adventurous stitcher. Hardanger is available in 22-count; linen in coarse (Cork linen is 9 stitches per one inch); medium (Dublin linen is 12 stitches per inch); and fine (Belfast linen is 16 stitches per inch). Even-weave linen has threads that are the same thickness and space apart. The latter is ideal for table linen and gives 12 stitches to the inch.

Plain-weave fabric

Only those fabrics with a regular, grid-like design such as gingham and striped or perhaps regularly spaced spotted designs are suitable for cross-stitch. The fabric should be sturdy enough to take solid areas of stitching without puckering or distorting; for this reason, loosely woven or knitted fabrics are not suitable for cross-stitch.

If the plain-weave fabric you wish to use is not marked with a grid-like design you may consider using the "waste canvas" technique. With this technique, a piece of canvas is tacked over the plain-weave fabric and the cross-stitch design is worked over both the canvas and the underlying fabric. More information on waste canvas is later in this chapter.

Canvas

Canvas is made up of horizontal and vertical threads that when woven together form evenly spaced holes between the threads. Most canvas is made from stiffened cotton, although soft linen and very fine silk gauze are available for particularly detailed work. Rigid plastic canvas with a coarse weave is suitable for less detailed designs that use thicker threads.

Three types of canvas are available: single (mono) canvas, interlocked canvas, and double (Penelope) canvas. Double canvas is considered the most suitable canvas for cross-stitch, being softer and having finer individual threads than the individual threads of a single canvas of the same grade. The more experienced cross-stitcher uses canvas, so unless you have done quite a bit of cross-stitching, it would be best to use Aida or linen fabric.

THREADS

There is a huge range of threads available in every imaginable shade, from silks and cottons to wools and synthetics, from fine to heavy-weight yarns. Some threads are twisted and are therefore meant to be used as a single thread, while others are made up of strands that can be divided and used singly or else combined with other strands of different colours or weights.

While the choice of thread is individual, it is important to match the thread to the background fabric. For example, if the thread is too fine then the fabric will show through, and if the thread is too coarse then the stitches will be cramped and bulky. Generally, cottons and silks are used for plain and even-weave fabrics, while wools and heavy-weight cottons are used for canvas.

The following are the four most commonly used cottons. **Stranded cotton** is the most useful of the embroidery yarns — it is a loosely twisted, high-lustre thread with six strands that can be divided for fine work. **Pearl (perle) cotton** cannot be divided but comes in three different weights and has a good colour range. **Danish Flower thread** is non-mercerised cotton with a matt finish. One strand of this is equal to two of stranded cotton and it comes in an extensive colour range. **Broder cotton** is a smoothly spun thread which is not usually divided.

NEEDLES

Three types of needles are used, depending on the background fabric. **Tapestry needles** have large eyes and

FABRIC, THREAD AND NEEDLE CHART

Fabric	Thread	Needle
Fine, plain-weave	Stranded cotton: 1, 2 or 3 strands	No. 8 Crewel for 1 or 2 strands, No. 7 for 3
	No. 8 Pearl cotton	No. 6 Crewel
	Broder cotton	No. 7 Crewel
Medium, plain-weave	Stranded cotton: 2, 3 or 4 strands	No. 8 Crewel for 2 strands, No. 7 for 3, No. 6 for 4
	No. 8 Pearl cotton	No. 6 Crewel
	No. 18 Broder cotton	No. 7 Crewel
Fine, even-weave	Stranded cotton: 1 to 6 strands	No. 25 Tapestry for 1 or 2 strands, No. 24 for 3, No. 23 for 4, No. 21 for 6
	No. 8 or No. 5 Pearl cotton	No. 23 Tapestry for No. 8 cotton, No. 21 for No. 5 cotton
	No. 18 Broder cotton	No. 24 Tapestry
Medium even-weave and canvas	Stranded cotton: 3, 4 or 6 strands	No. 24 Tapestry for 3 strands, No. 23 for 4, No. 21 for 6
	No. 8 or No. 5 Pearl cotton	No. 23 Tapestry for No. 8 cotton, No. 21 for No. 5 cotton
	No. 18 Broder cotton	No. 24 Tapestry
Coarse even-weave and canvas	Stranded cotton: 4 or 6 strands	No. 23 Tapestry for 4 strands, No. 21 for 6
	No. 5 Pearl cotton	No. 21 Tapestry

blunt points and are used to prevent threads from splitting. They come in a range of sizes from No. 18, the heaviest, to No. 24, the finest.

Most cross-stitch is done using a size 24 needle, using two strands of thread. Should this vary, a design will usually say what to use. To work on Belfast linen and Hardanger you could use a size 26, and for a fine design, you would work in one strand.

Needles have a larger than normal eye to take the various number of strands and the point is blunt. This is to enable the needle to separate the threads of the fabric and not go through them. This gives a neater, closer design.

SCISSORS

A pair of small embroidery scissors with pointed blades is essential for clipping threads. Another larger pair is also useful for cutting fabric.

THIMBLE

A thimble will protect your middle finger as you push the needle through the fabric. The best thimbles to use are made of metal ones with flat tips.

EMBROIDERY FRAMES AND HOOPS

Cross-stitch designs with areas of closely worked stitches are apt to pucker if the fabric is not supported in some way. An embroidery hoop or frame, which keeps the work taut and the fabric threads at right angles to each other, will minimise puckering and distortion and will make the holes marginally larger and easier to find.

Embroidery hoops consist of two plastic, wood, or metal circles, one

slightly smaller than the other. The fabric is placed over the smaller circle and then the larger circle is placed over the fabric. The fabric is gripped between the inner and outer circles and the tension is maintained by means of a screw on the outer ring (Fig. 3). To protect delicate fabrics the inner circle may be bound with cotton tape, however, it is a good idea to remove the fabric from the hoop if you intend stopping work for any length of time. To do this, simply undo the screw and remove the outer hoop.

Fig. 3. Using an embroidery hoop

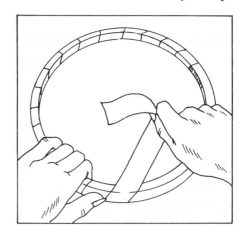

1. Tape with cotton to prevent damage to delicate fabrics and stitches.

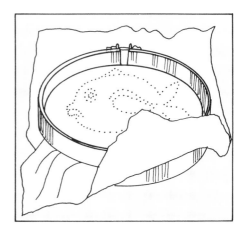

2. Place the fabric over the inner ring. Fit outer hoop over the fabric and adjust the screw so that the fabric is kept taut.

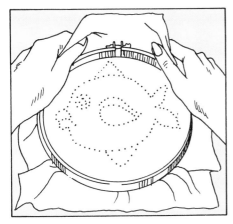

3. Working your way around the ring, press down over the fabric, pulling the fabric with your fingers as you go. When the fabric is taut and even, tighten the screw.

If the rings of the hoop cover an area of fabric already worked with cross-stitch, the pressure may damage the stitches. This damage can be minimised by placing a sheet of acid-free tissue paper over the entire fabric, placing the fabric in the hoop and then tearing away a hole in the paper where you wish to work (Fig. 4).

If your fabric is really too large for an embroidery hoop then it may be

Fig. 4. Using tissue paper with an embroidery hoop

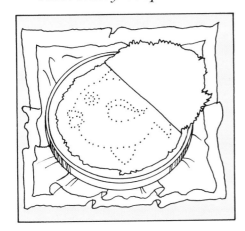

To reduce damage to fine fabrics and stitches, cover the fabric with tissue paper before placing it in the hoop. Tear away some of the paper to reveal working area.

more time saving to use a frame that can accommodate the entire piece of fabric at one time. There are two sophisticated frames on the market: the rotating frame and the slate frame, both of which are adjustable and which stretch the work very evenly. Both of these frames consist of top and bottom rollers with webbing attached, and two side pieces secured with nuts, screws, or pegs. The rotating frame allows for the fabric that has already been worked to be rolled out of the way (Fig. 5) while the slate

Fig. 5. Rotating frame

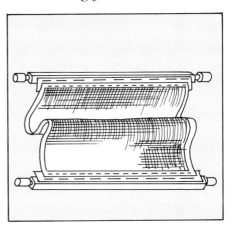

1. Top and bottom of canvas is stitched to the webbing.

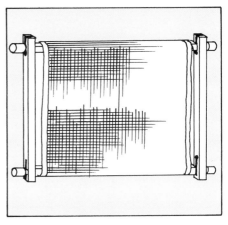

2. Insert the four ends of the side arms by loosening the nuts on the side arms. Make the fabric taut by turning the rods and then tighten the nuts on the side arms.

15

frame keeps the entire piece of embroidery on view at all times (Fig. 6). Adjustable frames may be purchased from specialty needlework stores.

Fig. 6. Slate frame

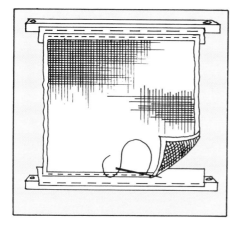

1. Hem the edges of the fabric to prevent fraying, then stitch the top of the canvas to the webbing on one rod, working from the centre outwards. Repeat on the other rod.

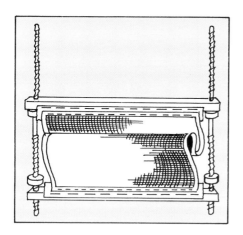

2. Fit the two locking nuts to the centre of each side arm. Slot the side arms into the holes of the top and bottom rods and slide the locking nuts towards the rods.

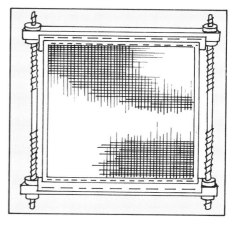

3. Draw the rods along the side arms to extend the canvas fully. Push the nuts close to the rods on both sides of the top and bottom rods. This will hold the canvas taut.

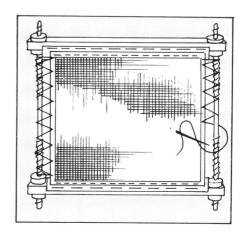

4. Oversew between the side arms and edges of the canvas, to hold the fabric tight at either side. Ensure that the tension is evenly distributed over the canvas.

EXTRAS

There are many other items that you will find useful at the creative, planning and preparatory stages of cross-stitch, such as graph, tracing and ordinary paper, coloured pens and pencils, chart markers, hands-free magnifiers and so on. Most of these will be unnecessary with ready-made kits but are essential if you intend to design and make an original.

Learning the Techniques

Before you begin your cross-stitch piece, give some thought as to whether the piece will be framed; if so, you will need to add at least 5 in (13 cm) of extra fabric on each side to allow for the framing process. If the item is not going to be framed, then 3in (8 cm) will be sufficient. When cutting the fabric, make sure that you follow the grain line or threads. Finish off the raw edges of the fabric with either hand or machine hem stitch or machine zigzag, or else use masking tape to seal the edges of stiff canvas — this will prevent fraying. Finally, locate the centre point of your fabric by folding it in half horizontally and finger pressing a fold at this point. Do the same along the vertical axis and then baste along the horizontal and vertical centre lines with large stitches in a contrasting colour (Fig. 7). This will give you the centre of the fabric. It is from the centre of the fabric that you will start stitching the design, working from the centre of the design.

It is worth spending some time before you start work organising your embroidery threads. If you have purchased a kit, the threads will

Fig. 7. Basting the centre lines of the fabric

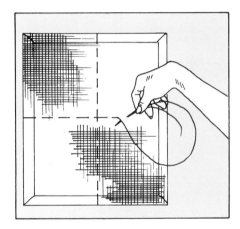

probably have been supplied ready cut into suitable lengths. Sort the threads and place each colour into a thread organiser, which can easily be made from a piece of stiff cardboard into which a series of holes have been punched along one side. Keep a record of the dye lot numbers of each skein, so that if you run out of a particular thread you will be able to match the colour exactly.

If you have purchased skeins of thread, you may either pre-cut the thread into lengths and place them in the thread organiser, or else wind the thread on to a bobbin or piece of cardboard and cut the thread as you require it; either way the threads should be more than 15 in (38cm) long. While it may be tempting to use longer thread lengths, you will end up wasting time untangling threads and untwisting stitches and the thread may fray or lose its sheen after passing too many times through the fabric.

Depending on the type of thread you have chosen you may need to separate the thread into individual strands. Separate the strands as required rather than prior to commencing work, because once they are separated they will tangle easily.

CHARTING DESIGNS

Cross-stitch designs on even-weave and canvas fabrics are most often rendered in chart form, that is, each stitch is represented by one square on a piece of graph paper. The chart is interpreted by counting the threads in the fabric. Because the fabric remains unmarked, changes can be made to the design while the work is in progress.

To transfer a design to chart form you need ready printed, graphed tracing paper. Lay this over the design, making sure it is centred and secured by tape. Trace the outlines of the design with a fine felt pen, adjusting the outlines to fit the squares of the graph, or if you prefer, use a symbol system for each square to indicate colour, for example a dot for green, a cross for red and so on.

If you cannot obtain ready graphed tracing paper, lay the design on a glass-topped table with a strong light source underneath. Place ordinary graph paper over the top of the design so

that you can see the design through the graph paper. Proceed as for the previous method.

WORKING FROM CHARTS

The key to all counted cross-stitch is the chart from which you transfer the design to the fabric. One square on the chart represents one stitch and you will note that the squares have different symbols in them. These represent the different colours making up the design. Notice the 'colour key' on your chart. Look at the first symbol and then look at the chart and see where the colour occurs.

The size of the chart IS NOT the size of the finished design. The count of stitches to the inch refers to the squares on the graph. If there is no size on the graph then count the number of squares between the two outside stitches on each side and divide by the size of the fabric eg: if you count 140 stitches and you are using AIDA 14, then the design will be 10in (25cm) wide. Count the stitches down as well as across to give you both the measurements.

On some charts, you will notice that there are two symbols in one square. This means that one half of the stitch is in one colour, and the other half in the other colour.

On your graph there should be arrows at the centre of each side. These indicate the middle of the graph. Draw a line from the left arrow to the right arrow and from the top arrow to the bottom arrow. Where they intersect is the middle of the graph. You now have a starting point for the work.

Floral images have been included in this early sampler.

Stitched on linen fabric

Two bookmarks finished in a different way — and stitched on different fabrics. See pages 72-73, 74, 79 for instructions.

Add a pretty design, like these
two ducks and a delicate satin bow,
to your child's pillow case.
See pages 66-67 for instructions.

A baby's bib is made more
appealing with the addition of
small teddy bears cross-stitched
onto an Aida band. See pages 62-63
for instructions.

Acorns on an Aida band on a hand towel. See pages 84-85 for instructions.

HOW TO DETERMINE THE FINISHED SIZE AND FABRIC REQUIREMENT

The following details will help you to work out the finished size of a cross-stitch design, and the amount of fabric you need, according to the count of the fabric you propose to use.

A.   Many commercial charts have counts already printed on them; if your chart does not, you must carefully count the stitches. Determine the maximum width and height of the design in stitches, eg: 120 stitches wide by 235 stitches high.

B.   Choose a suitable fabric and note the number of *stitches* per inch. Remember, if you are using linen rather than a block-form fabric like Aida, that the number of stitches to the inch is *half* the number of threads to the inch.

C.   Divide the number of stitches in the design by the number of stitches/inch in the fabric. This gives the dimensions of the finished work in inches.

   For the equivalent in centimetres, multiply these figures by 2.54.

e.g.: On 14-count fabric:

$$\frac{120}{14} = 8\,^{8}/_{14}\text{in} \ (8.57 \times 2.54 = 21.8\text{cm})$$

$$\frac{235}{14} = 16\,^{11}/_{14}\text{in} \ (16.78 \times 2.54 = 42.6\text{cm})$$

   Your design on 14-count fabric measures approximately 8½ x 16¾ in or 22 x 43cm.

D.   Experiment with different fabric counts until you achieve the size you want the finished piece to be.

E.   Add a border of 2in (5cm) of unstitched fabric on each side to determine the amount of fabric required.

   Having completed the chart it is worth covering it in clear contact plastic, both to protect it from accidental rips or spills and to make it easier to roll up and store.

   Unless the grid size of your graph paper exactly equals the thread count of your fabric, the chart you have just made will not represent the size of the finished cross-stitch piece. The finished size will depend on whether each stitch is worked over one thread or a number of threads as well as on the gauge of canvas or the thread count of the fabric being used. For example, the graph measures 50 squares by 50 squares, the fabric has a thread count of 20 (that is, 20 threads per 1in (2.5cm), and you have decided to work each stitch over two threads. This means there will be 10 stitches per 1in (2.5cm) and the finished design will measure 5 x 5in. (13 x 13cm). Don't forget when calculating how much fabric you will need, to add at least 3in (8cm) all around, and 5in (13cm) if the work is to be framed.

ENLARGING AND REDUCING DESIGNS

Sometimes you will need to enlarge or reduce a design motif to an appropriate size before you can chart your design. The easiest solution to this problem is to take your design to a professional photocopying service and have it enlarged or reduced according to your specifications. If you do not have access to a photocopier, follow the grid technique shown in the diagrams (Figs. 8 and 9).

Fig. 8. Enlarging a design

1. *Trace the design onto the centre of a sheet of paper*

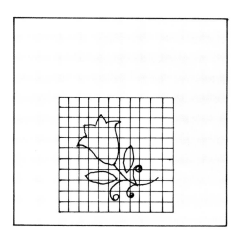

2. *Draw a grid over the design*

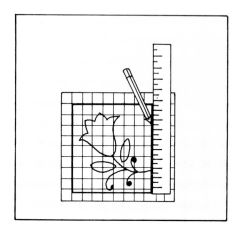

3. *Define the outside edge of the design to the size you prefer*

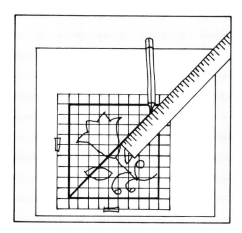

4. *Tape the grid to the lower left-hand corner of a bigger sheet of paper, then draw a corner to corner line diagonally across the area of the design. Take the line beyond the grid*

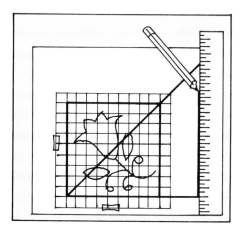

5. *Extend the bottom line of the design area to the preferred width. Draw a straight line up to form a right angle, extending the line so that it meets the diagonal*

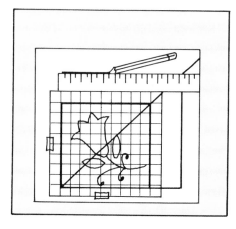

6. *Using the finished width and height worked out in the previous step, draw in the remaining two sides of the rectangle*

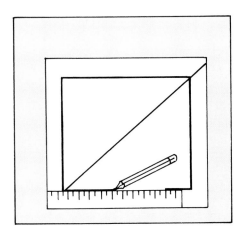

7. *Remove the grid. Fill in the area that was covered by the grid and complete the enlarged rectangle*

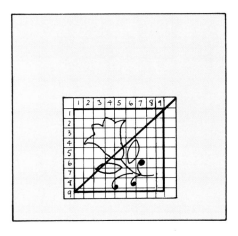

8. *Number each square across the top and down the side of the design on the grid as above*

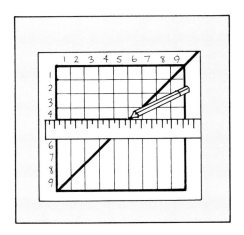

9. *Count the squares within the marked grid and divide the bigger rectangle into the same number of squares*

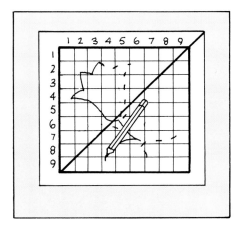

10. *To reproduce the design, copy the lines within the small squares onto the corresponding squares of the bigger grid*

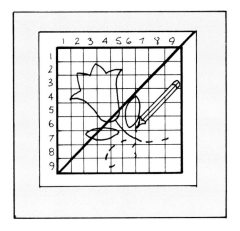

11. *A hint to make copying easier for you: place a mark where the design lines go across a square and join the marks*

Fig. 9. Reducing a design

1. Trace the design onto the middle of a sheet of paper

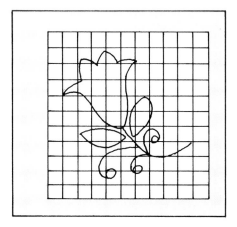

2. Draw a grid over the design. Mark the outside edges of the design area to the size you think looks best

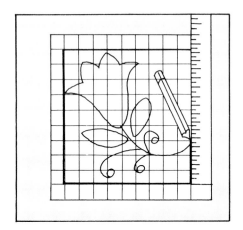

3. Mark perimiters of design to desired size

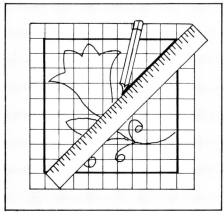

4. Draw a line diagonally from corner to the corner of the design area which you have marked off on the grid. Tape a smaller sheet of paper to the lower left-hand corner

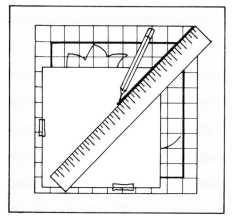

5. Extend the diagonal line at the upper right-hand corner of the grid straight down to the lower left-hand corner of the taped sheet of paper as above

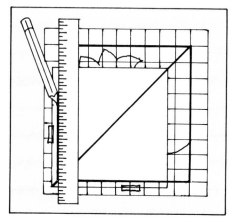

6. Carry on the bottom line of the design area until it meets the diagonal line, and join the intersecting point with the outside edge line at the left side to form a right angle as above

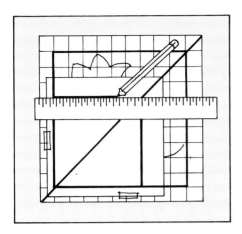

7. *Mark off the width you want the design to be at the bottom of the small sheet and draw a line up at a right angle to meet the diagonal. Mark the height you want at the left and draw a connecting line at the top*

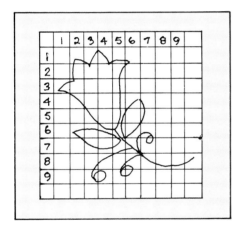

8. *Along the outside edge of the design on the large grid, number each square as shown in the illustration above*

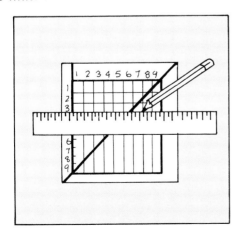

9. *Count up the number of squares within the marked grid, and then divide the small rectangle into the same number of squares*

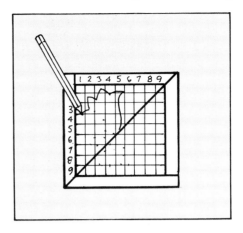

10. *To reproduce the design you must copy the lines within the large squares onto the equivalent squares of the smaller grid*

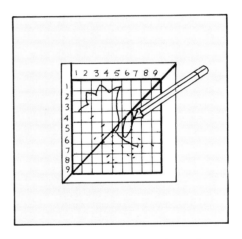

11. *Hint to make copying easier: place a mark where the lines of the design go across a square and join the marks*

TRANSFERRING DESIGNS

The simplest way of transferring designs is by using an iron-on transfer. Simply place the transfer face down on the fabric and rest an iron, on a low heat setting, on it for a few moments. Do not glide the iron over the transfer. Lift up a corner to ensure that the design is taking.

BEGINNING AND ENDING THE THREAD

A knot that is intended to remain at the back of the work should never be used in cross-stitch, because after mounting it may show through. When making the first few cross-stitches, ensure that they are worked over the thread at the back of the work (Fig. 10).

Fig. 10. Working over method

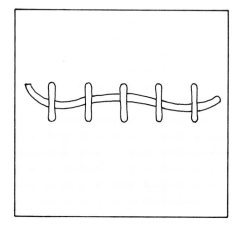

Beginning a thread.

To start stitching, hold a piece of thread about one inch long at the back of the fabric, and work the first stitches over this thread to secure it. Alternatively, leave a piece of thread the length of one and a half needles at stitching, thread the needle with this tail and weave it through the back of the stitches. Cut off the waste knot on the right side of the work and continue with the stitches. To finish off a thread, embed it in a row of stitches at the back of the work by sliding the needle behind approximately 1 in (2.5cm) of stitches and trimming off the remaining thread

(Fig. 11). Each colour should be finished off into itself, that is, green into green, and yellow into yellow.

Fig. 11. Finishing off a thread at the back of the work

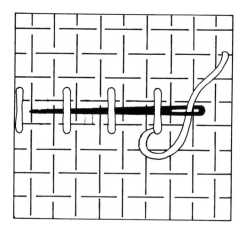

When ending off, do not push the needle under the whole of the stitch at the back as it will pull the stitches tight and show a difference in tension. Run the needle through the top of the threads.

Try not to finish off too many threads in the same place as this could create a lumpy appearance to the finished work.

MAKING A CROSS-STITCH

There are two ways of making a simple cross-stitch. The first method, involves making each stitch individually, that is, each stitch is completed before moving on to the next stitch (Fig. 12). The second method is used on plain and even-weave fabrics and consists of working a row of diagonal stitches in one direction, followed by a row of diagonal stitches in the other direction over the top of the first row (Fig. 13). With either method, ensure that the top diagonals are always worked in the

Fig. 12. Cross-stitch — making each stitch one by one

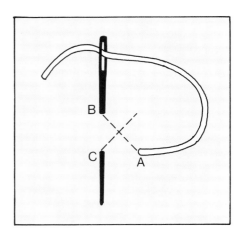

A. Start up from the wrong side at point A. Insert needle at point B. Half the cross should be made on the right side of the fabric. Bring needle to C from wrong side of fabric.

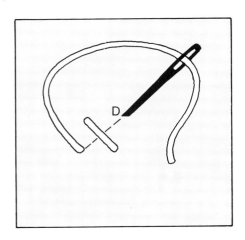

B. Insert needle at D to complete each cross.

Fig. 13. Cross-stitch — making a row of stitches

1. Make a row of half crosses, following the numbers in order.

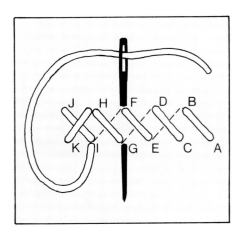

2. Complete the crosses, following the numbers as illustrated.

same direction. For an illustrated guide to cross-stitch variations and other useful stitches, refer to 'An A-Z of Stitches'.

It is important to maintain an even tension in cross-stitch. If your tension is too tight, the fabric will pucker and distort, and if it is too loose the shape of the stitch will be lost.

WASTE CANVAS

This is a special type of material with a loose weave usually in counts of 8, 10, 14 or 18. It is a firm canvas unlike Aida or linen. This medium allows you to put a cross-stitch design on to a T-shirt, sloppy Joe or sweat shirt. Be adventuresome and experiment. You can put designs on anything. If you are putting a design onto a towel, do not go for the thick, fluffy pile. The thickness makes it too hard to pull the threads out.

How to use waste canvas

Cut the piece of canvas about 2.5cm larger all round than your design. Position it on the garment and tack around the outside of it. Make sure that it lies flat. If it is a large piece, then you should do the centre stitching to help you find the centre. Work over the threads of the canvas and make sure that you do not pull the stitches too tight. They should sit neatly on the fabric. When you have worked the design and tidied the back of the work carefully cut away the waste canvas around the design — not too closely. You are best to use a pair of tweezers to remove the canvas threads. CAREFULLY pull out the threads one by one until only the design is left on the garment. If the fabric of the garment is a stretch or very fine fabric, you may need to use a backing fabric to ensure that the design stays in shape, or to strengthen the area.

COMMON MISTAKES AND HOW TO FIX THEM

It is normal for some twisting of the thread to occur while stitching. If the thread is tightly twisted, let the needle and thread hang down from the work and it will unravel itself (Fig. 14). Do not continue to work with twisted thread,

Fig. 14. Unravelling a twisted thread

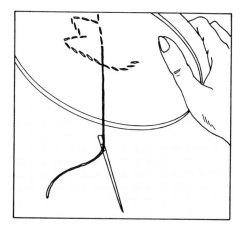

since this will change the overall sheen or patina of the work and will also have an effect on the tension and shape of your stitches. Continually twisting threads may mean that you have pre-cut your threads too long.

One of the most common errors made by beginners is that of changing the direction of the stitches. This can be avoided by placing a symbol at the top of your canvas, for example a "T". If the work is always held with the "T" at the top, the direction of the stitches should remain the same.

If an error in stitching is made over just one or two stitches, it is possible to remove the stitch simply by unpicking it gently (do not pull or tug).

Do not worry too much about missed stitches. If in doubt about the placement or colour of a particular stitch, leave it out. When the finished cross-stitch piece is held up to the light, the missing stitches will show and they can easily be added.

To help preserve your work in progress: keep your cross-stitch piece clean by storing it in a pillow case or a large clean cloth when you are not working on it; wash your hands each time you sit down to stitch and do not pat or stroke the work or let others do so; and avoid wearing clothes that will shed fibres onto it while you are working.

CLEANING

Unless you have been absolutely meticulous about keeping your hands and your work clean, the finished cross-stitch item will probably need to be washed. If you have used washable fabric and threads, the piece can be gently handwashed in cool, soapy water. Do not use washing detergents. If you suspect that the colours may run then add a little white vinegar to the water, which will help set the colours. Never pull, tug, wring, or squeeze the work while it is wet, as this will pull the fabric out of shape. Rinse well in a few changes of cool water. Roll the piece in a towel and press gently to remove excess water. Do not hang out to dry or spin dry.

Very delicate cross-stitch may be washed by placing it on top of a piece of cloth and using a sponge to press cool, soapy water into the work. Rinse a number of times using the same

technique and then place a dry cloth underneath the work and press gently with another piece of dry cloth. Leave it until dry. If the work is smoothed out well before drying then it shouldn't need ironing.

If the piece is not washable, for example if you have used silk thread, it may be dry cleaned. Do not have the piece pressed by the dry cleaners, however, as this will squash the stitches and the texture of the embroidery will be lost.

PRESSING

Plain- and even-weave fabrics worked on a hoop or frame will generally suffer only minor distortion, so a gentle pressing while the fabric is still damp from washing will usually be sufficient to restore the fabric to its original shape. Place a folded dry towel on the ironing board and lay the damp cross-stitch face down over it. Cover it with a dry pressing cloth and iron the work very lightly, just allowing the iron to touch the pressing cloth. Do not exert any pressure downwards on the cross-stitch piece, as this will flatten the stitches. Pull the work gently into shape as you iron. If you have not washed the piece it can still be ironed, except use a damp pressing cloth instead of a dry one.

HARDBOARD MOUNTING

To mount on hardboard, use mounting board or chipboard separated from the fabric by a barrier of acid-free rag paper (available from art supply shops). Stiff cardboard or foam board can also be used. The most common method is to mount the work directly on to the hardboard and lace it firmly across the back of the board. If using this technique, the fabric should first be oversewn or hemmed to prevent fraying when the lacing is pulled tight (Fig. 15). Instead of lacing, masking tape may also be used to hold the work in place on the board, although there is a risk that the glue on the tape may deteriorate over time. Batting

Fig. 15. Mounting on hardboard

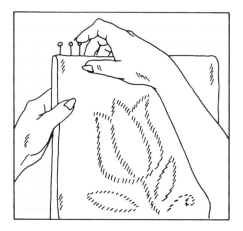

1. Place cross-stitch piece, face side up, over the hardboard. Pin the unworked edges of the fabric into the outside edges of the board.

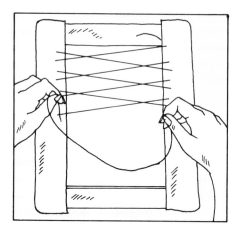

2. Turn the board over and with strong thread, lace the two opposing edges together with large interlacing stitches. Pull each thread tight as you go.

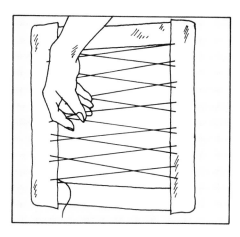

3. Remove the pins and make a knot at the beginning of the thread. Tighten the stitches by pulling on the thread as you go. The fabric should be fully stretched.

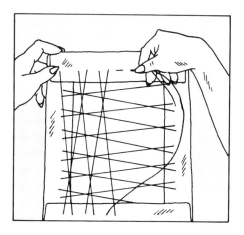

4. Repeat the lacing process on the other two sides. Make box corners with the ends of the fabric.

(wadding) may be placed between the hardboard and the fabric to give a padded effect to the work.

Another way of mounting on hardboard involves covering the hardboard with a fabric such as linen and then stitching the cross-stitch fabric to that fabric. Whilst more time consuming, this is a useful technique when mounting very delicate fabrics.

FRAMING

Ready-made frames are available from needlework and specialty shops in a variety of sizes and shapes to suit your finished piece, or you may choose to have a frame custom made by a professional picture framer. Whichever you decide, give some thought to whether or not you want glass in the frame; if so, you will need to ensure that the glass does not touch the item, both to avoid squashing the stitches and to allow some air circulation. Non-reflective glass is a better choice for display purposes; also, make sure that the back of the frame is well insulated from dust and dirt by backing the frame with heavy cardboard and then sealing the gap between the frame and the cardboard with masking tape (Fig. 16).

*Fig. 16. Sealing the back of the
framed piece*

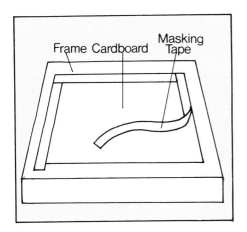

CROSS-STITCH CARE

The most important thing to remember is to avoid exposing the cross-stitch piece to fluctuations in temperature, humidity and light. Therefore, never place in direct sunlight, directly above a heater or fireplace, and keep it away from open windows. A mounted cross-stitch piece that is not kept behind glass may be vacuumed occasionally to remove dust and dirt, although if the fabric is very delicate then a fabric screen over the nozzle of the vacuum may be necessary to protect the threads from damage.

A FEW IMPORTANT THINGS TO REMEMBER WHEN DOING CROSS-STITCH

NEVER	use a knot
ANCHOR	thread at beginning and end of stitching
BRING	needle up in an empty hole and down in an unoccupied one — if possible.
NEVER	jump more than 4 stitches especially if no stitching is going over it
BE SURE	all your top crosses are in the same direction
TRIM	threads as you go to keep the back tidy

Creating Samplers

ENGLISH SAMPLERS

While the origin of the sampler is unknown, there is evidence from Asia that they may have been in use as early as the ninth century. The earliest European reference to samplers occurred in the English royal household account book of 1502, with an order for a yard of linen to make a sampler for Queen Elizabeth of York. The oldest surviving example of a dated sampler is also English, and was stitched in 1598. It was made by Jane Bostocke and was probably intended as a gift for Alice Lee, a little girl whose name is also mentioned on the sampler. Other examples ascribed to the Elizabethan period include canvas trial pieces with designs suitable for table carpets and long cushions and possibly some of the long, narrow linen samplers worked in rows of cutwork, whitework and silk embroidery.

Before the printing revolution, making a sampler was the only way of remembering newly learned stitches and needlework patterns. Once the stitch or motif was worked on fabric it was available for future reference when particular designs were needed for decorating household items or clothing.

The development of printing around the middle of the fifteenth century, making available numerous pattern books had a major influence on the spread of patterns and designs for embroidery over the next 100 years. Books of designs were also translated from one language to another, allowing a free flow of ideas between countries.

Printed patterns meant that the purpose of samplers changed somewhat; from being a way of remembering stitches, the sampler became a record of a needlewoman's skill and versatility, a way of demonstrating her technical virtuosity with needle and thread. In addition, working a single motif allowed her to experiment with colour progressions and thread quantities, an important factor given the cost of fabric and yarn. The preponderance of samplers based on designs with alphabets and numbers suggests that they may also have had an educational purpose. Most of the samplers were worked by girls as young as five and demonstrate the rigorous training and high level of technical expertise demanded of very young children in times gone by.

A great many samplers from the seventeenth century have survived, most of which fall into one of two basic stylistic groups: the band sampler and the spot sampler. The band sampler was long and narrow and designs were worked in horizontal rows, often in complex progressions of colour and design. Spot samplers, on the other hand, consisted of single motifs worked at random over the piece of fabric. Both styles of sampler were worked on a long, thin piece of linen, the shape of which was probably dictated by the size of the looms of the period. When complete, the samplers were usually rolled up in the form of a scroll and kept in the needlework basket until required.

During the eighteenth century a change occurred in the style of the samplers. The formidable seventeenth-century sampler, with its rigid exposition of technique, gave way to an emphasis on pictorial representation in a style heavily influenced by Chinese and Indian designs. Linen was exchanged for woollen canvas and samplers became squarer. The range of stitches tends to be rather limited in most of the surviving examples from this period and suggests that the designs or motifs used on them were becoming more important than the stitches used to create them. Map samplers were produced in large numbers, using mainly cross-stitch on linen backgrounds. The accuracy of the maps indicates, perhaps, that geography, rather than embroidery, was the subject being studied. The fact that fewer samplers were embroidered by young girls may also indicate that embroidery was becoming a less important element in their education.

Samplers were almost entirely supplanted by Berlin wool work in the nineteenth century, and those that were worked show the influence of the new craze in the use of three-dimensionally shaded motifs, a feature of this style. In the latter half of the century samplers all but disappeared in England and were not revived until the 1930s, when a publication by Mrs Archibald Christie entitled *Samplers and Stitches* created new interest in traditional embroidery techniques.

EUROPEAN SAMPLERS

European samplers by and large mirrored the styles seen in England. In Italy, band samplers were very popular and were used to demonstrate a variety of cutwork, drawn threadwork and white on white embroidery. Northern European samplers used fewer stitches, with cross-stitch being the most popular. German embroiderers created both band samplers and a small, square type of sampler that used a single letter of the alphabet surrounded by smaller, geometric motifs. Mexican and Spanish samplers were very decorative and used bright colours and flamboyant designs on large pieces of fabric.

AMERICAN SAMPLERS

The earliest examples of American embroidery, not surprisingly, show the influence of English styles that were imported with the early settlers. The earliest dated piece, commenced in the 1630s and completed in 1655, was made by Loara Standish, and while it demonstrates a high level of technical skill it is not distinguished by any stylistic differences between it and its English counterparts of the same period.

Academies for young women used the sampler as a way of teaching basic sewing, darning and embroidery techniques, while others were more decorative and used pictorial motifs and selections of verse with fancy embroidery stitches.

It was not until the eighteenth century, when the population of the colony had tripled, that American embroidery began to take on its own identity. This is in part attributed to Mary Daintree, an eight-year-old embroiderer who was the first to use a border in her sampler and thereby enlarged its function from solely one of study or reference to one of display as well.

The latter part of the century saw the first memorial sampler, a particularly American motif to commemorate the death of Abraham Lincoln. From then on, samplers were often used to record the deaths of family members, public figures, or sweethearts. The family tree sampler also began to occupy a place of prominence on the walls of American homes. Story-telling samplers, with naturalistic renditions of landscapes, houses and people in contemporary costume, were popular.

As in Europe and England, the number of decorative stitches used in samplers diminished, and by the end of the eighteenth century many samplers show cross-stitch used alone with stylised or geometric motifs. The advent of the sewing machine in the middle of the nineteenth century, and the inexpensive printing of richly patterned fabrics heralded a decline in sampler embroidery until this century. Its revival has been due as much to an interest in the historical information it provides as to its aesthetic appeal.

DESIGNING A SAMPLER

Designing your own sampler gives you a great deal of freedom in the choice of motifs, colour, stitch size, style and proportion. You need not be limited to traditional patterns or arrangements of motifs, but a sampler based on an eighteenth-century design, for example, can certainly lend an air of old world charm to a room. If you wish to replicate the feel of an old sampler, museums with a section on textile history or books on the history of embroidery will give you a good starting point. Try looking at old wallpaper designs or the patterns used on antique china; often these motifs can be adapted for embroidery. Flowers formed an integral part of many of the old samplers, and there are plenty of designs in kit form currently on the market that could be used as the basis of a sampler. Flowers can also be used to convey hidden messages, as each species has its own significance, for example, a rose means love, a lily purity, and so on.

The human form can be conveyed very successfully in embroidery, and works particularly well in the context of a family tree or story-telling sampler. Attention to details such as dress or physical characteristics of the figures will lend originality to the design.

Fruit and vegetables would make a novel basis for a sampler designed for the kitchen, while birds and animals combined with a nursery rhyme would be suitable for a young child's room.

A traditonal-style sampler would include an alphabet or a piece of verse, decorative designs such as flowers, foliage, or geometric shapes arranged symmetrically around the central motif and a border to enclose and contain the design. Your name or initials and the date of completion of the work can also be included, usually at the top or bottom of the sampler.

The colours you choose should reflect the style of design you have chosen. Obviously very bright colours, metallic threads and sequins will look totally out of place in a sampler based on seventeenth-century motifs, although they may well complement a contemporary sampler that uses abstract designs and a broad range of unusual stitches. These are only general guidelines, however, and unorthodox combinations may work very well if properly thought out and planned in advance.

Design Elements
Alphabets and numbers

Alphabets and numbers form the basis of numerous traditional samplers and seemed to be used, not only as a way of developing embroidery techniques but as a method of learning basic literacy and numeracy skills as well. They may have originally be practised because most household linen was marked with the initials or monograms of the head of the house.

Many different stitches can be used to execute letters and numbers, although cross-stitch is the style most traditionally associated with this motif. It produces well-defined shapes and can be used in single lines or to create solid areas of colour.

Mottos· and lettering

Verse, poems, sayings, religious and moral tracts, proverbs and so on provide the basis for most lettering seen on traditional samplers. Anything with a meaning that is designed to be read should be planned very carefully, since the lettering needs to be well spaced in order to be legible. Do not just measure the space between letters, since each letter reacts with its neighbour in a different way. Move the letters around until the spacing seems right overall. The use of contrasting thread against a neutral coloured background is important, as is the choice of a not overly ornate stitch. Old English lettering may look attractive, but it is quite difficult to read when embroidered.

Monograms and ciphers

A cipher consists of two letters arranged ornamentally over one another. A monogram also uses two (or more) letters, the upright stroke of one letter also forming the upright of the second, so that neither letter is complete. The letters may be distinguished from one another by using different colours, stitches or thread weights. There are many commercially available kits with decorative letter motifs that could be combined to form monograms or ciphers, or you could design your own.

Family trees

Early examples of family tree samplers indicate the these were undertaken over a long period of time with spaces left for the date of death, although this rather practical approach may not gel with our modern day sensibilities.

Family tree samplers can be extremely complex affairs with information about family relations going back several generations, or they may be restricted to your own immediate family: mother, father and offspring. Instead of family members' names, initials combined with human figures can look attractive as can monograms, family shields and crests combined with purely decorative motifs.

Houses

The family home was one of the most common motifs used in American samplers. Domestic architecture was recorded faithfully, as were features of the surrounding landscape, family members, pets, garden furniture and domestic animals such as chickens and horses.

Kit forms of cottage-style homes are readily available, or you may prefer to represent your own home. In order to do this, you will need a photograph or accurate drawing of the house which can be transferred to graph paper in the way suggested in Chapter 3. For added realism, make sure that the embroidery threads match the actual colours of your house.

Borders and corners

A border acts as a frame for the rest of the design and therefore needs to be in harmony with it. Traditional samplers used geometric motifs or stylised designs of vines, flowers, or plants, and there are plenty of examples in books or available in kit form. If you wish to design your own, look for inspiration in associated crafts such as quilting and patchwork or in the designs of Persian or Chinese rugs, where border motifs form a strong part of the overall design.

A simple border may consist of just two or three rows of cross-stitch worked in contrasting or complementary colours. More complex designs require that you pay some attention to the corners, since the design may not turn a corner easily. A mirror can be used to design the motif so that it flows continuously around the corner (Fig. 17).

Fig. 17. Using a mirror to design the border corner

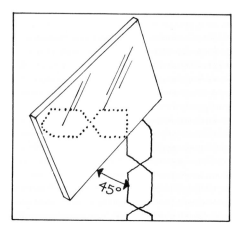

Experiment with the angle until you find a point at which to make the corner turn.

An attractive addition to a terracotta plant pot, stitched on an Aida band in a terracotta-coloured thread. See pages 64-65 for instructions.

This place mat and serviette make an attractive addition to any table. See pages 80-81 for instructions.

39

Snowflakes in ice blue make a charming pattern for a shelf trim stitched on Aida fabric. See pages 86-87 for instructions.

Individual fruits feature on the top of these jam jars. See pages 68-69 for instructions.

Romance is in the message of this sampler. See pages 92-95 for instructions.

Alternatively, the design used for the borders may stop short of the corners and a different corner motif inserted, or compensating stitches may be used in order to fit the design within the corner angle (Fig. 18). If the border is a complex one, textural interest can be added by varying flat with raised stitches, or by using areas with stitching to contrast with areas devoid of stitching.

Fig. 18. Different ways of completing a corner design

Before you start to actually design your own sampler, spend a few moments gathering your thoughts on the type of sampler that you aim to stitch.

Will the symbols balance each other in the general design? Do the colours harmonise — or are there too many? Sometimes it helps to simplify a design. Too many symbols, names and borders can be confusing, so it is often best to leave out something. You can always use it in your next sampler.

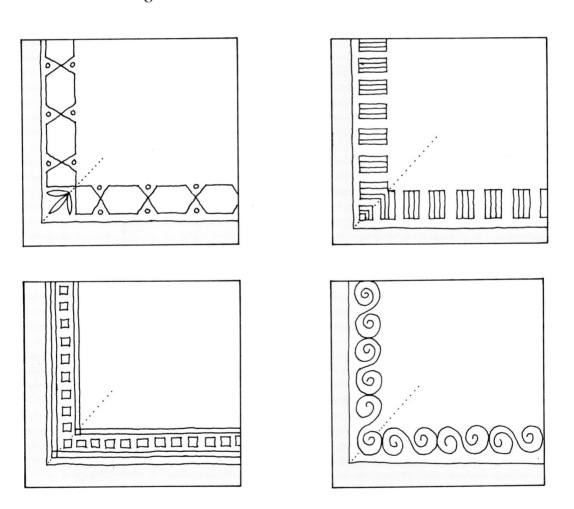

SYMBOLS

The symbols found in many samplers have a historical meaning. Following is a list of the various symbols and an explanation of their meaning.

The Peacock — Eternity; immortality

Fruit basket — Fertility

Ship — Noah's Ark

Hourglass — The perishableness of life

Crown — The crown of life, elevation, and dignity

Heart — Love, and also devotion to another

Tree — The Tree of Life; the Tree of Knowledge

Lamb — Christ as the sacrificial lamb

Wreath — Symbol of eternity (possibly also a symbol of victory)

Dog — Faithfulness

The Deer — Yearning for Christ

The House — The gate to the Kingdom of Heaven, may also be representative of Salomon's temple in the holy city of Jerusalem

The Key — The keys to the Kingdom of Heaven — St Peter the Apostle's key

The Star — The symbol of the Star of Bethlehem

Candlestick, three-branched — The parishioners

THE ALPHABET

An alphabet is an essential item in any cross-stitcher's stitching vocabulary. The alphabet is used in samplers, and to sign the stitcher's initials in the corner of treasured pieces. Here is a cross-stitched alphabet, and one to use in backstitch (for the initials).

An A–Z of Stitches

In this chapter you will find a variety of embroidery stitches which are sometimes used in conjunction with a basic cross-stitch. As you become more experienced, you may like to experiment and incorporate a few into your designs. The illustrations and accompanying how-to-do-it text are easy to follow, so have confidence in your stitching ability and, with a little practise, you will soon be able to stitch them perfectly.

BACKSTITCH *(PW, EW, C)*

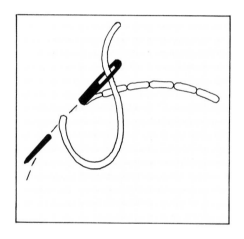

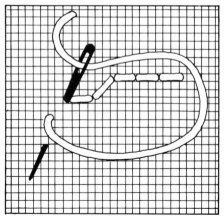

Another outline stitch, backstitch looks like machine stitching and may be worked on all fabrics. On canvas, the stitch should follow the line of the shape it is outlining.

BASKET STITCH *(PW)*

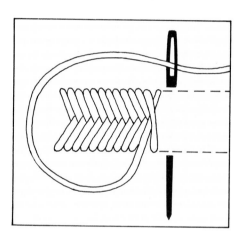

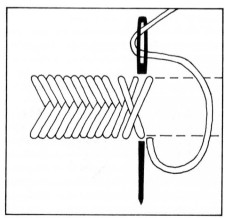

This stitch gives a braided effect and can be used to give an open or closed finish.

BASKETWEAVE STITCH (C)

BULLION STITCH

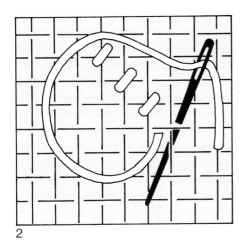

1

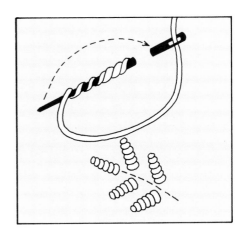

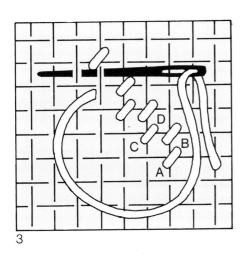

2

Pick up a backstitch, the size you want the bullion stitch to be, bringing the point of the needle out where it first came out. Do not pull the needle right through the fabric. Then twist the thread around the point of the needle as many times as necessary to equal the space of the backstitch. Hold the left thumb on the coiled thread, then pull the needle through. Still holding the coiled thread, you then turn the needle to the original insertion position (see illustration) and insert it in the same place. Pull the thread through until the bullion stitch lies flat. It is best to use a needle with a small eye to allow the thread to pass through the coils more easily.

3

This stitch is similar to continental stitch except that it is worked on the diagonal. It may be used with any type of canvas.

CONTINENTAL STITCH (C)

CROSS-STITCH (ALTERNATE) (EW)

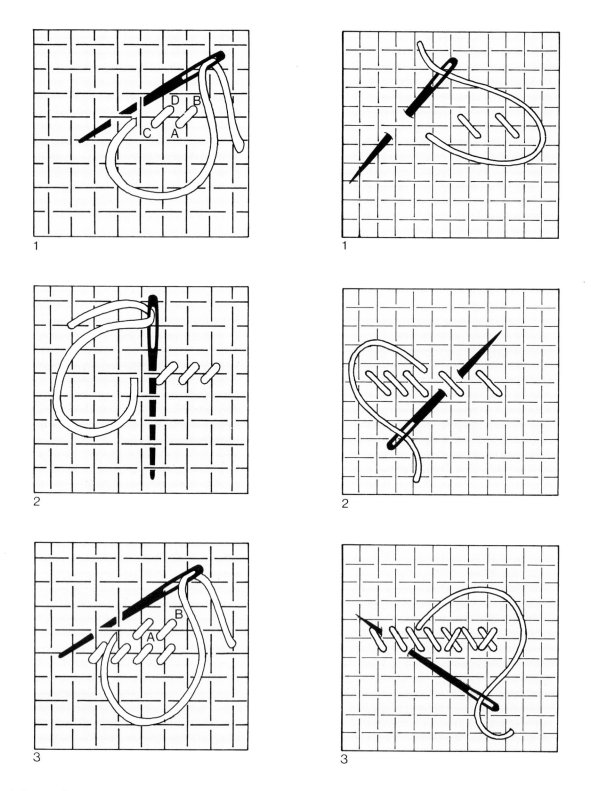

A form of tent stitch, continental stitch may be worked on single as well as double canvas. It uses more thread than the half-cross stitch and is therefore a sturdier stitch.

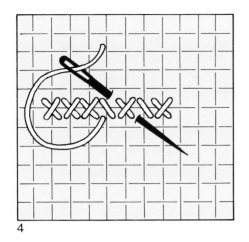

4

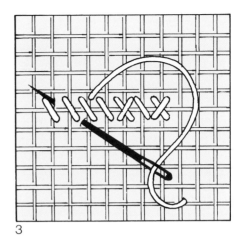

3

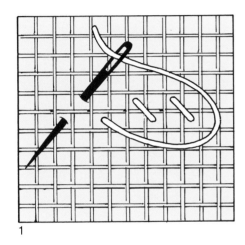

1

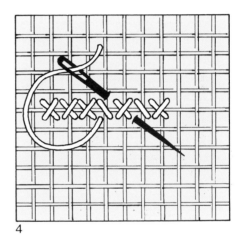

4

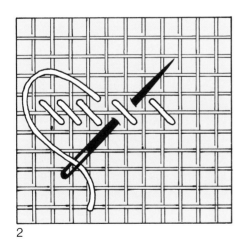

2

This method of making the cross-stitch ensures an even tension. Four journeys are required to finish a row of cross-stitch, two for the lower diagonals and two to finish the crosses.

47

CROSS-STITCH (DOUBLE-SIDED)
(PW, EW)

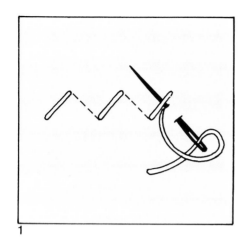

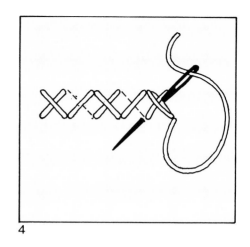

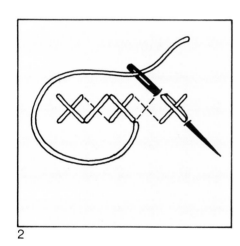

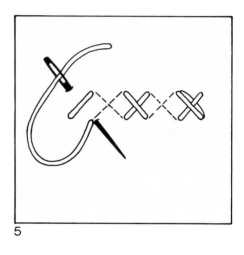

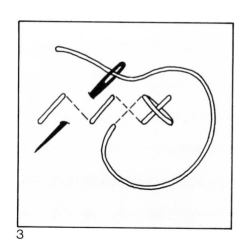

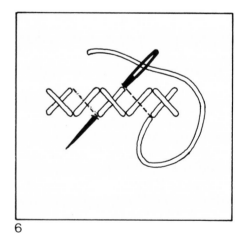

A useful stitch for fine fabrics where the back of a normal cross-stitch would show through. Because the stitch is the same on both sides it can be used on reversible fabrics.

CROSS-STITCH (DIAGONAL) *(C)*

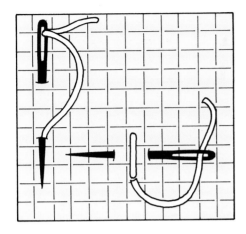

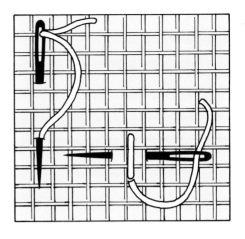

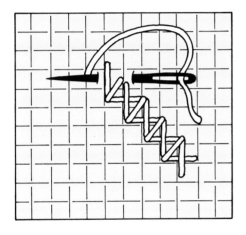

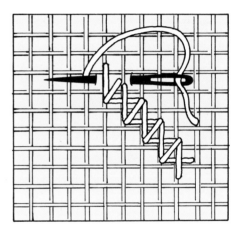

Use the diagonal cross-stitch on canvas as a filling stitch, or if a striped effect is desired.

CROSS-STITCH (LONG ARMED)
(EW, C)

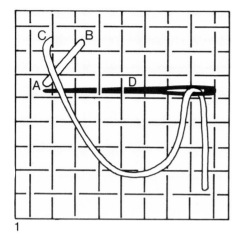

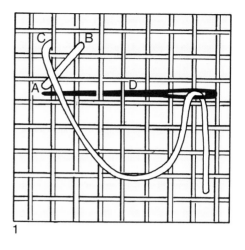

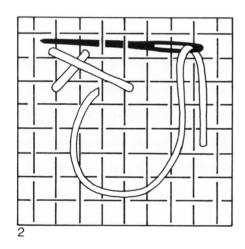

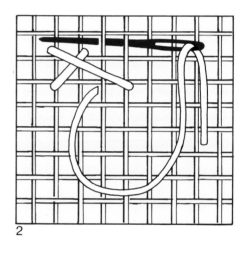

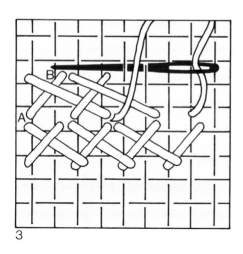

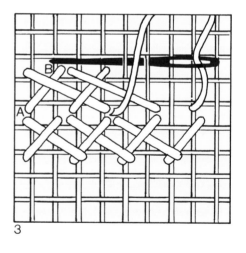

This stitch is always worked from left to right, with each long arm running over twice the number of threads as the short arm. End each row with a short arm and then the canvas should be turned upside down and the work started again from left to right.

CROSS-STITCH (OBLONG) (C)

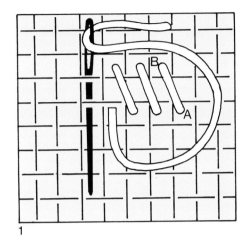

1

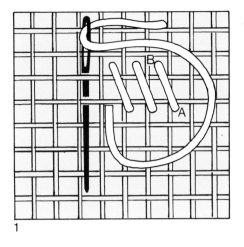

1

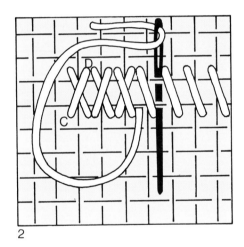

2

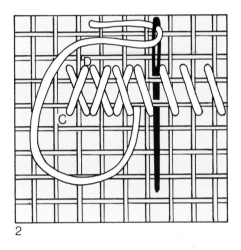

2

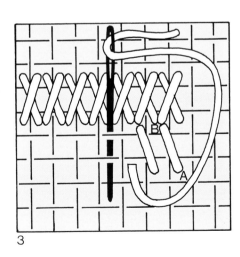

3

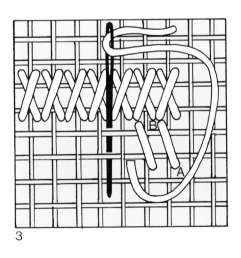

3

This stitch is made in the same way as ordinary cross-stitch, except that the space between A and B is two crosswise threads by one lengthwise.

51

CROSS-STITCH (UPRIGHT)

(EW, C)

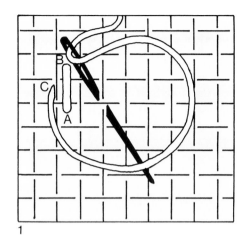

1

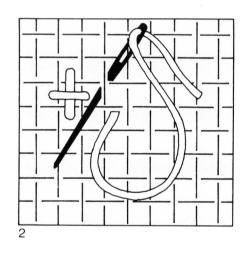

2

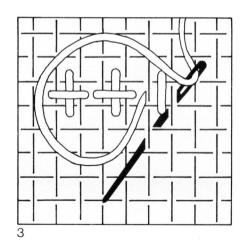

3

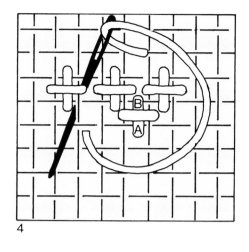

4

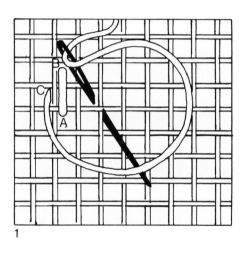

1

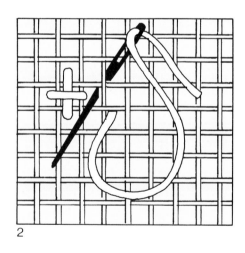

2

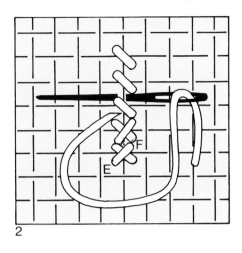

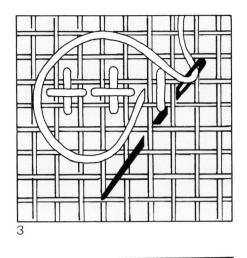

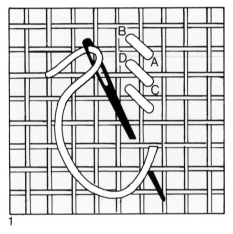

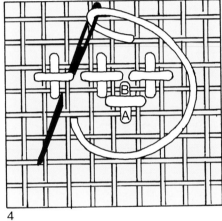

This stitch is worked from left to right and then right to left on the following row. Make sure that the tops of the second row of stitches share a canvas hole with the horizontal stitches of the previous row (step 4).

CROSS-STITCH (VERTICAL) *(EW, C)*

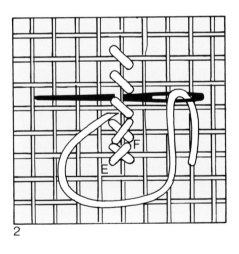

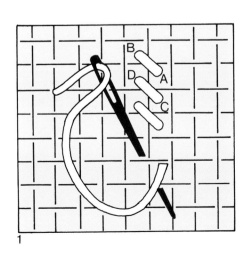

Commence the stitch at the top and work from A to B, then C to D and so on. Complete the cross by working from bottom to top. The next row of stitches should start to the left of those already made.

FERN STITCH (C)

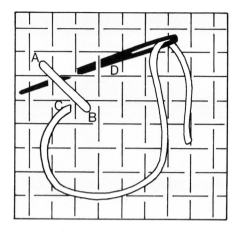

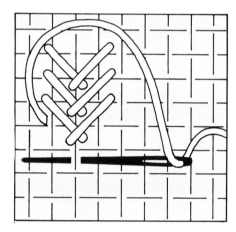

Fern stitch forms plaited vertical ridges and should be worked on double canvas. Each row must be worked from the top of the bottom of the canvas and a new row should be started to the right of the one just completed.

FRENCH KNOTS (PW, C)

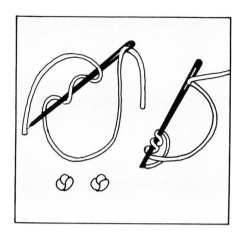

Bring thread to right side. Hold thread with the left thumb and encircle the thread twice with the needle. Twist the needle back to the starting point of the thread and insert needle, pulling the thread to the back of the fabric.

HEM STITCH

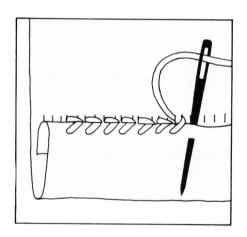

After completing your embroidery, finish the edges with a 1cm wide hem. Draw a thread along the inner edge of the hem and hem stitch.

HALF-CROSS STITCH (C)

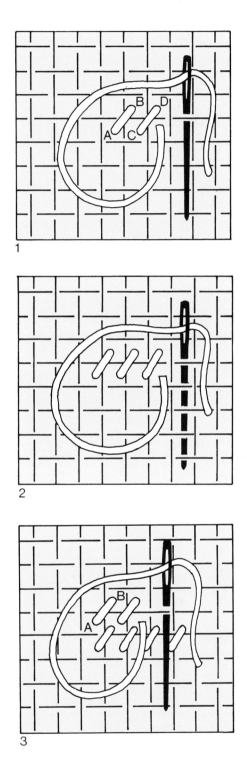

1

2

3

HERRINGBONE STITCH (EW, PW, C)

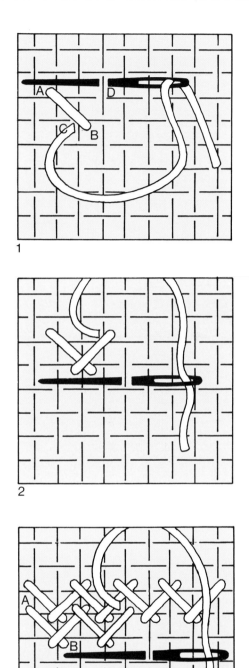

1

2

3

This stitch is a form of tent stitch which is best worked on double canvas. At the end of each row, leave the needle at the back of the work, turn the canvas upside down and form the new row next to the one you have just done.

Work all rows of herringbone from left to right. The fabric must be turned therefore when starting a new row. Begin each row in the hole below where the stitch starts in the row above (step 3).

HERRINGBONE (DOUBLE)
(EW, PW, C)

HERRINGBONE (CLOSED)
(EW, PW)

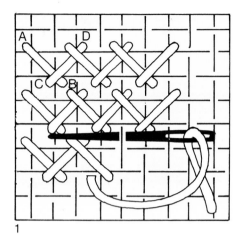

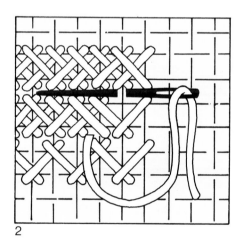

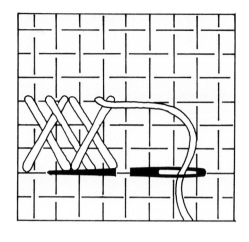

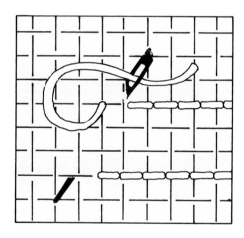

This stitch consists of a row of ordinary herringbone with a second row usually in a different colour, worked over the top.

This stitch is worked in the same way as ordinary herringbone except that the diagonals touch at the top and bottom.

A sampler that will always be close to any grandmother's heart.
See pages 98-101 for instructions.

Lavender sachets are a great idea for gifts for family and friends.
See pages 88-89 for instructions.

A cross-stitch design is always a charming addition to a gift. See pages 82-83 for instructions.

This butterfly was stitched onto a child's T-shirt using waste canvas. See pages 96-97 for instructions.

This decoration will be the centre of attention on any Christmas tree. See pages 102-103 for instructions.

LEVIATHON STITCH *(EW, C)*

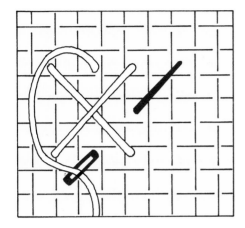

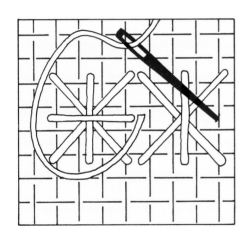

SATIN STITCH *(EW, PW, C)*

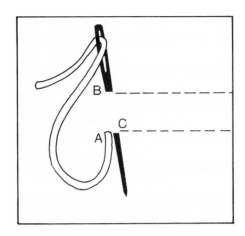

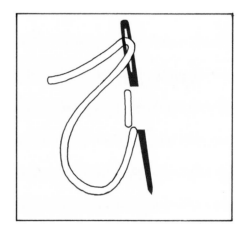

This stitch consists of two crosses, an ordinary cross-stitch covered by an upright cross. Each stitch is worked individually and alternating colours may be used to create a chequerboard effect.

Satin stitches consist of long, straight stitches placed close together. They may be worked straight up and down, or slanting.
When worked at differing angles they can create the effect of light and shade.

RUNNING STITCH *(PW, EW, C)*

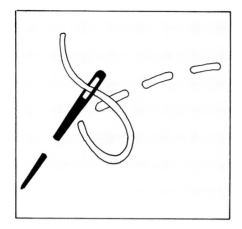

C	— CANVAS
EW	— EVEN WEAVE
PW	— PLAIN WEAVE

Running stitch is used as an outline stitch for solid areas of other stitching.

20 Projects to Stitch

*T*he 20 counted cross-stitch projects in this chapter have been especially designed and stitched for this book. Janette Heaven working in association with Di Cross designed 18 of the items. These projects begin with easy designs and simple charts, and work their way through to more complicated, but still easy to follow, chart designs. The child's sampler and "To The House of a Friend the Way is Never Long" sampler were designed by Louise Wilkinson. Each of the 20 projects is accompanied by a list of the fabric and thread colours to use, plus an exact chart to follow. You may alter the colours used in the designs if you wish, but do be careful to keep to similar shadings of the new colour as specified in the original thread colours. For example, if you decide to use blue, not green, and it reads 'mid green' then use mid blue.

1. Baby's Bib

MATERIALS

1 piece of white 14-count Aida border band, 4in (10cm) longer than the width of the bib.
Baby's bib (purchased or made)

THREADS

1 skein light brown
1 skein dark brown
1 skein black
1 skein red

INSTRUCTIONS

The motifs are centred and stitched onto the Aida band. When completed, press to the back both end raw edges. Place in position on the bib front and stitch in place.

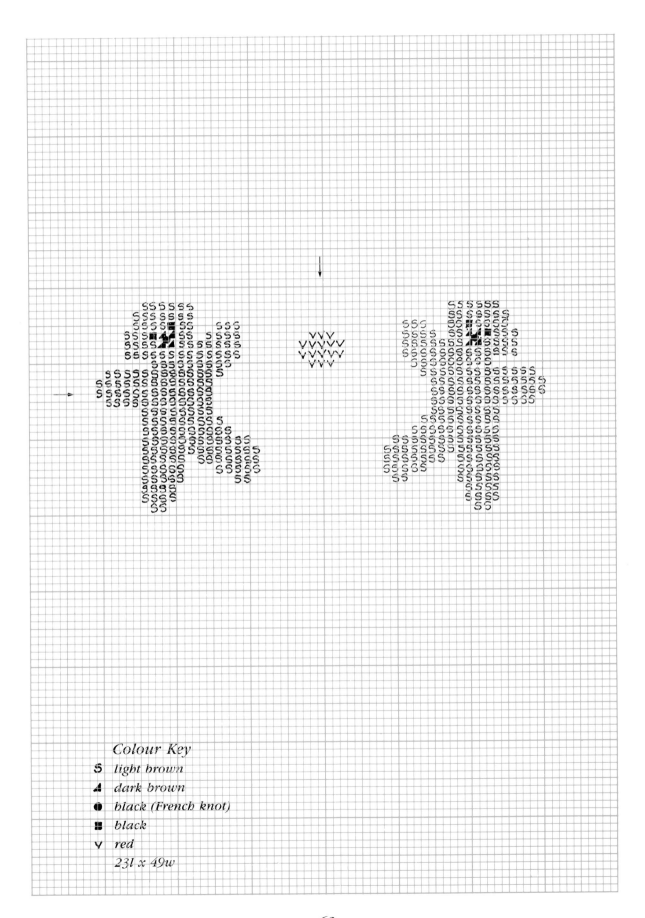

Colour Key

5   light brown
4   dark brown
●   black (French knot)
▉   black
v   red
    23l x 49w

2. *Decorative Flower Pot Trim*

MATERIALS

1 piece of cream 14-count Aida 6in (15cm) wide and a length equal to the circumference of the pot plus an overlap of 2in (5cm) Velcro strip

THREADS

1 skein dark terracotta
1 skein green
1 skein light terracotta

INSTRUCTIONS

Cross-stitch the motifs in the centre of the strip, repeating the design as many times as required.

Mark a border two rows above and below the finished embroidery with large tacking stitches.

Fold back the fabric along these lines, tuck under the raw edges and slip stitch the hem. At both ends, hem the raw edges, and attach a small length of Velcro. This means the trim can be removed for washing, or can be re-used when you change the pot.

Wrap the band around the pot tightly and secure with the piece of Velcro.

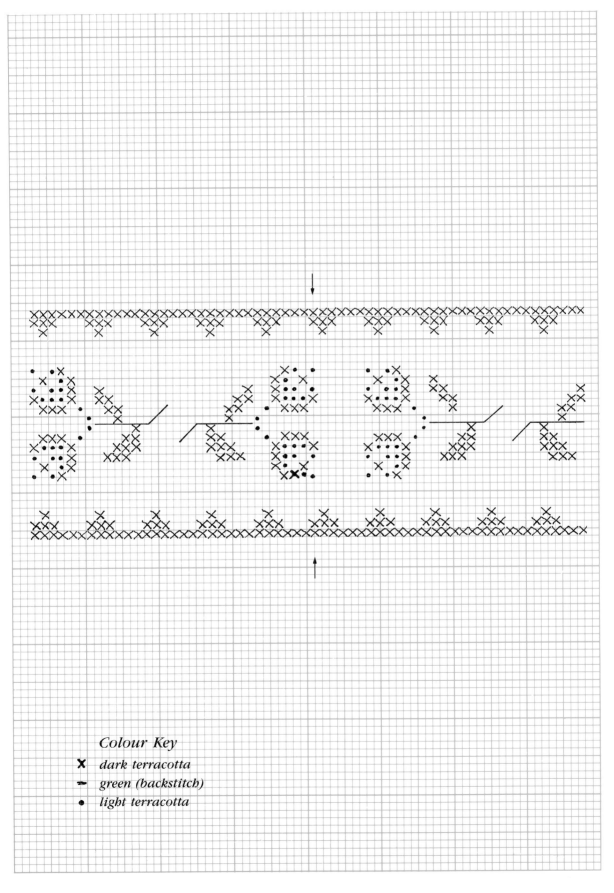

Colour Key

X dark terracotta

— green (backstitch)

• light terracotta

3. Baby Pillow Case Trim

MATERIALS

1 piece white 14-count Aida 5in (12.5cm) wide, and 2in (5.5cm) longer than required for the width of the pillow case.
White baby pillow case
1yd (1m) of $^1/_8$in (3mm) wide yellow satin ribbon

THREADS

1 skein each of the following colours:
  black
  pink
  blue
  green
  yellow
  orange

INSTRUCTIONS

Cross-stitch the ducks down the centre of the strip, repeating the design either along the length or only twice as shown and adding a small bow to give the design a soft look.

When stitching is completed, weave the narrow ribbon down both sides of the strip, 5 rows out from the last cross-stitch. Weave over three square and under two, making sure both sides match each other with corresponding over and under weaves. Go slowly to prevent the ribbon twisting.

Fold back a hem two rows away from the ribbon border and iron. Repeat at the top and bottom of the strip so that the Aida fits exactly the pillow case width, and then stitch in place.

Cut an 8in (20cm) length of ribbon, tie a small bow and, with a few stitches, attach it in position on the lower half of the trim, as in the photograph.

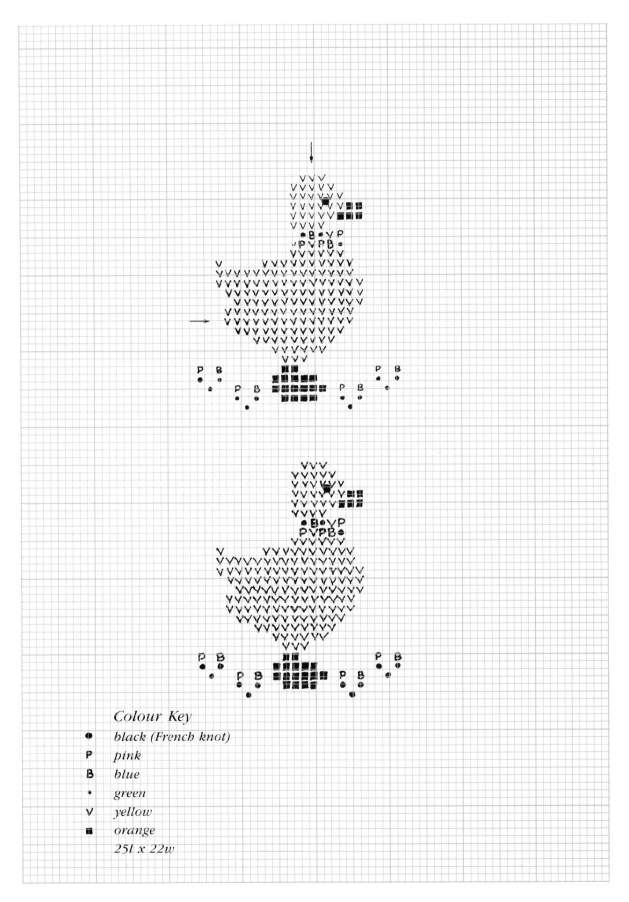

Colour Key

●	black (French knot)
P	pink
B	blue
•	green
V	yellow
▦	orange
	25l x 22w

4. Jam Jar Covers

MATERIALS

1 piece of 10in (25cm) square of cream linen

Tracing paper to make pattern

½ yd (.5m) cream bias binding or 1in (2.5cm) wide anglaise trim

12in x ¼ in (40cm x 6mm) wide cream ribbon

Compass to draw circle for pattern

THREADS

1 skein each of the following colours:
    brown
    white
    light plum
    medium plum
    olive green
    medium cherry red
    dark cherry red
    red
    green

INSTRUCTIONS

Make a pattern on the tracing paper of a 9in (23cm) circle for large jars or a 7in (18cm) one for smaller jars.

Place this pattern on the worked cross-stitch with the design centred, then cut out the circle.

Enclose the raw edge of the linen circle with the cream bias binding or stitch on a lace trim.

Place the completed cover on top of the jar and tie a length of ribbon around the cover and onto the neck of the jar.

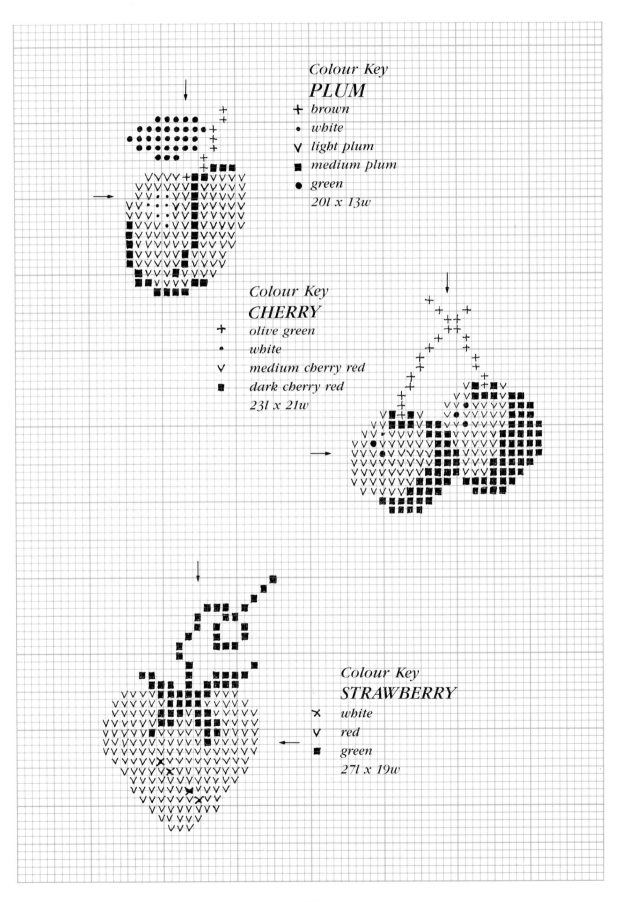

Colour Key
PLUM
+ brown
• white
∨ light plum
■ medium plum
● green
20l x 13w

Colour Key
CHERRY
+ olive green
• white
∨ medium cherry red
■ dark cherry red
23l x 21w

Colour Key
STRAWBERRY
✕ white
∨ red
■ green
27l x 19w

5. Child's Sampler

This lovely design celebrates the birth of a baby. The colours can be altered to suit your baby's room — the blue and yellow of this design, though, is fresh and suits a baby of either sex.

MATERIALS

1 piece of 14-count Aida measuring 12in (30cm) x 14in (35cm)

THREADS

1 skein of mid blue
1 skein of light blue
1 skein of dark green
1 skein of mid green
1 skein of yellow

INSTRUCTIONS

Two strands are used for all cross-stitching, and one strand for all of the backstitching, using a no. 25 tapestry needle.

Find the centre of the chart, and the centre of the fabric piece, and begin, following the chart. 'Bless this child', the date, and the numbers along the bottom are backstitched.

The actual size of the design is 6 1/8 in (15.5cm) x 7 5/8 in (19.5cm)

Bless This Child

PATRICK

27.2.1991

ABCDEFGHIJKLMN
OPQRSTUVWXYZ

1234567890

Colour Key   **+** *light blue*   **✗** *dark blue*   **•** *yellow*   **○** *light green*   **—** *dark green*

6. *Here I Fell Asleep Bookmark*

MATERIALS

1 piece of Dublin linen measuring
3½ in (9cm) x 10in (25cm).

THREADS

1 skein red
1 skein yellow
1 skein orange
1 skein pale green

INSTRUCTIONS

The pale green is worked with one
strand of thread and as a half-cross
stitch only.

Allow ½ in (1.2cm) at the top and
side before you start working. Work
the border cross-stitch first, then work
the design. When finished, carefully
pull the threads away at the top and
bottom and sides up to the cross-stitch.

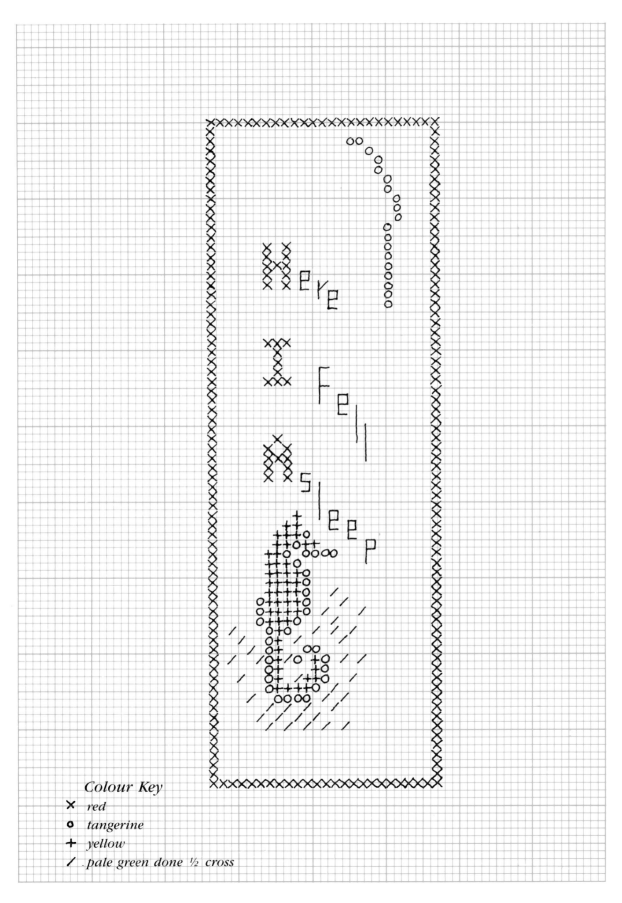

Colour Key

× red
○ tangerine
+ yellow
╱ pale green done ½ cross

7. *Happy Birthday Bookmark*

MATERIALS

1 piece Aida band measuring 10in (25cm)

THREADS

dark yellow
dark red
dark pink
dark blue
dark green

INSTRUCTIONS

Start working 10 rows down from the top in two strands of thread. When you have finished, fray the top down five rows and fray the bottom 10 rows.

Backstitch the balloon strings with one strand of blue thread.

The message in this sampler is one all readers will know. See pages 90-91 for instructions.

Cream damask, satin ribbon and a dainty cross-stitch design combine to make a lovely wedding pillow. See pages 104-105 for instructions.

An afternoon tea cloth featuring a lovely red rose is the project on pages 106-107.

A delightful sampler for a child's room is stitched in blue and lemon on Aida fabric, and is set in a thin metal frame. See pages 70-71 for instructions.

This cushion will make a lovely addition to any room. See pages 108-111 for instructions.

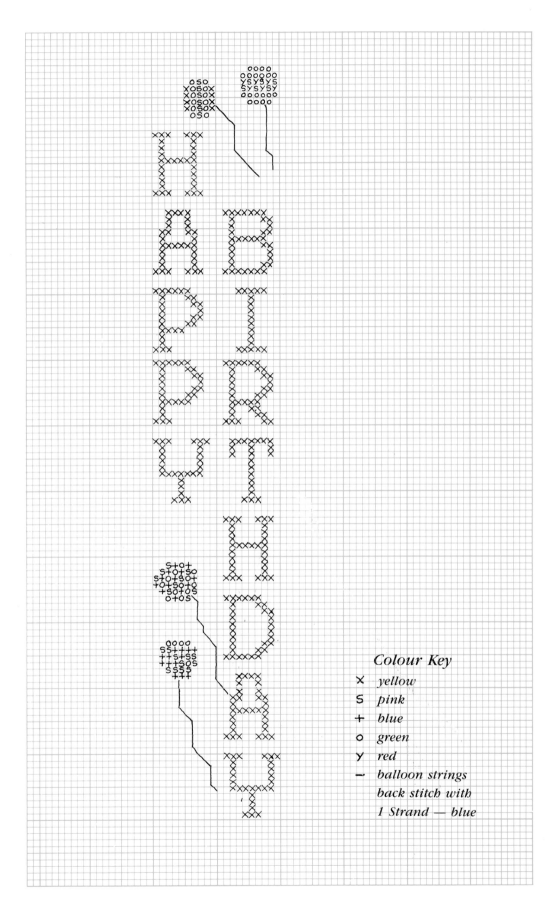

Colour Key

X	*yellow*
S	*pink*
+	*blue*
o	*green*
Y	*red*
—	*balloon strings*
	back stitch with
	1 Strand — blue

8. *Place Mat and Serviette*

MATERIALS

14-count Aida

THREADS

1 skein dark cotton pink
1 skein medium cotton pink
1 skein light cotton pink

INSTRUCTIONS

Cut one piece of 14-count Aida 12in (30.5cm) x 18in (45.5cm) and one piece 14-count Aida 12in (30.5cm) x 12in (30.5cm) for each place setting.

Hem carefully with ½in (1.25cm). Turn in five rows and turn in again keeping hem straight.

Place Mat

Border starts 15 rows from the edge. Work with the long edge at the bottom to ensure that all corners go the same way.

Serviette

Border starts 12 rows in from the edge.

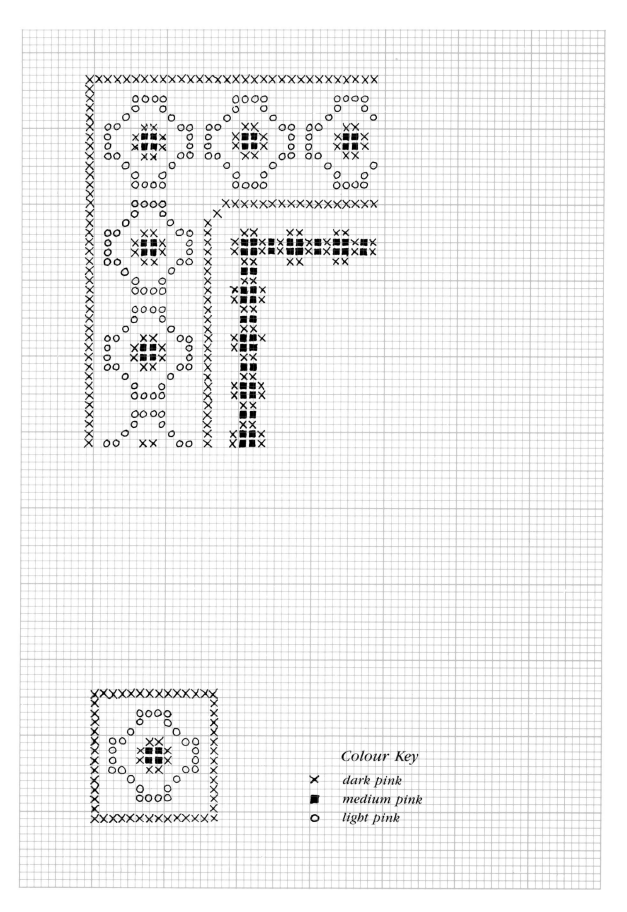

Colour Key

✗ dark pink
■ medium pink
○ light pink

9. *Easter Card*

MATERIALS

1 piece of 4in (10cm) square grey
14-count Aida
Small gift card with cut-out window
Glue

THREADS

1 skein dark yellow
1 skein yellow
1 skein black
1 skein orange
1 skein white

INSTRUCTIONS

After the Easter motif is complete, insert the worked fabric behind the window. Trim to fit and glue in place. Fold over the card flap to cover the back of the embroidery.

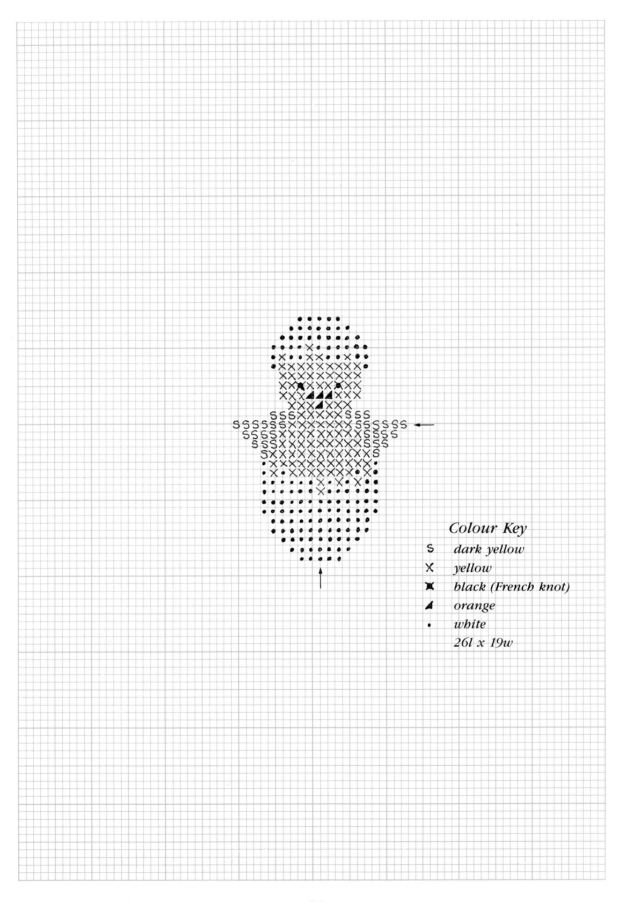

Colour Key

S	dark yellow
X	yellow
✖	black (French knot)
◢	orange
•	white
	26l x 19w

10. Acorn Hand Towel

MATERIALS

1 hand towel (cream)
1 piece of cream 14-count Aida
6in (15cm) x 16in (40.5cm)

THREADS

1 skein dark green stranded cotton
(back stitch)
1 skein of medium green stranded
cotton
1 skein of light green stranded
cotton
1 skein dark brown (stems)
1 skein of olive brown
1 skein of light old gold

INSTRUCTIONS

Find the centre of the fabric and
mark fabric accordingly. Starting with
the centre motif, work as per graph
with 2 strands of thread. The
backstitch around the leaves and for
the veins on the leaves is done with a
single strand. Repeat the motif on
either side of the centre one making
three in all.

FINISHING

Cut Aida to fit the width of the
towel allowing for ½in (1.25cm)
turnings. Make sure that the same
amount of cloth is on each end. Allow
6 rows top and bottom when turning
the cloth. Press the seam allowances in
and pin to the towel so that the ends
come to just inside the border of the
towel. This can be sewn by machine
but looks better if done by hand.

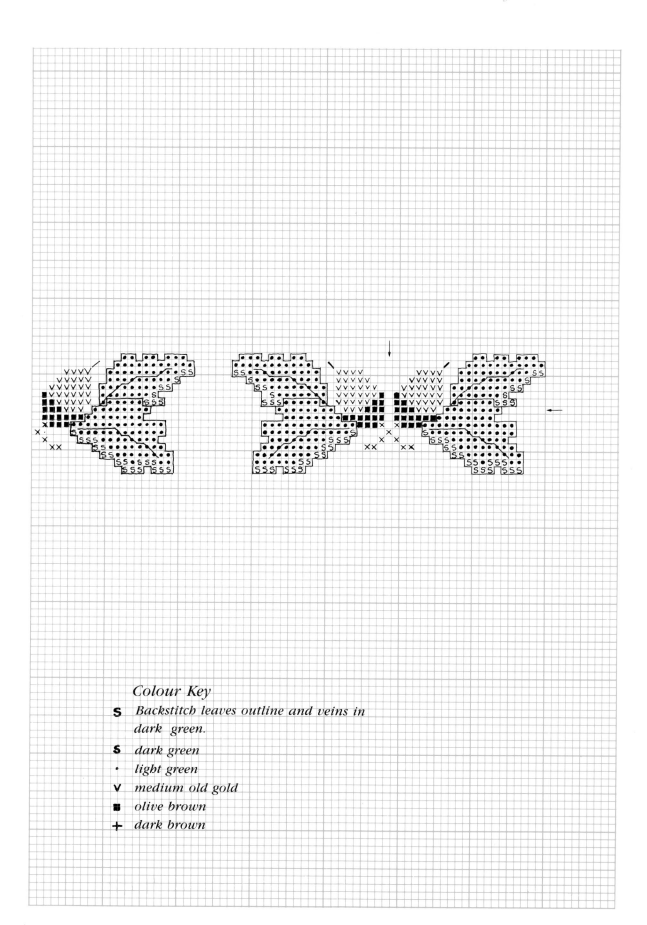

Colour Key

S Backstitch leaves outline and veins in
   dark green.

S dark green

· light green

V medium old gold

■ olive brown

+ dark brown

11. Shelf Trim

MATERIALS

14-count cream Aida fabric 6in (15cm) x 26in (66cm)
1 piece of calico fabric measuring the depth of the shelf x 26in (66cm)

THREADS

1 skein cornflower blue dark
1 skein gold

INSTRUCTIONS

Find the centre of the fabric and work first motif. Count 16 rows and start next motif on 17th row. (You can reduce the number of rows between each motif if you like).

There should be the same number of rows between each motif. The last motif should be a full motif, or half exactly to make the design balanced.

MAKING THE LIP

Turn Aida to 15 rows beyond last row of stitches on both sides and both ends. Turn up five rows and then turn up again and hem either by hand or by machine. Keep stitching straight and do not go through cross-stitch design.

Turn in ends and hem the same way.

Hem the two short sides and one long side. Place the unhemmed calico side and Aida right sides together and stitch a ½in (1.2cm) hem. Open out and press towards the calico and stitch the seam to the calico shelf lining.

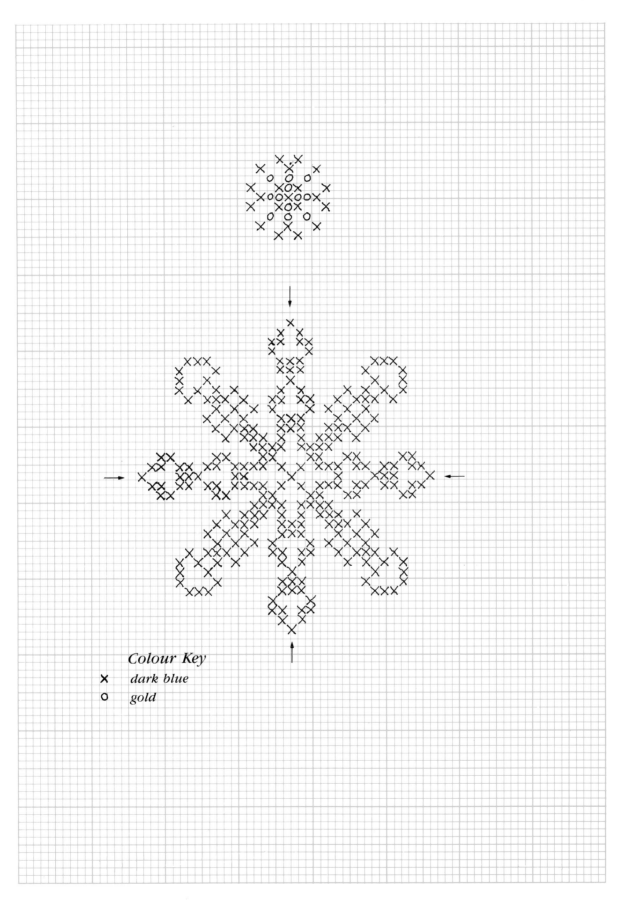

Colour Key

X   dark blue

o   gold

12. *Lavender Sachets*

MATERIALS

1 piece of 9in (22.8cm) x 6in (15cm)
rectangle of white 14-count Aida
12in (30cm) x ¼in (.6cm) wide ribbon
Dried lavender

THREADS

1 skein violet
1 skein dark violet
1 skein yellow
1 skein dark green

INSTRUCTIONS

Overlock or machine zigzag all raw
edges of the Aida rectangle. Visually
divide the area into four and
embroider the design in the bottom
right hand quadrant.

Fold the Aida fabric in half, right
sides facing to form the sachet. Stitch a
seam of three rows wide along the
bottom and up the side. Turn right side
out. Fold back a ¾in (1.8cm) hem
along the top edge, iron, and slip
stitch to secure.

Fill the sachet with dried lavender,
and tie with a length of ribbon,
finished in a bow.

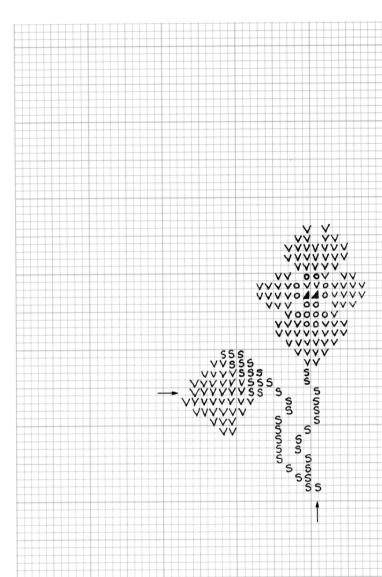

Colour Key

V   violet
o   dark violet
◢   yellow
S   dark green
~   dark violet (backstitch flower outline)
    22l x 14w

13. *To the house of a friend the way is never long*

This sampler has a friendly message delivered in a clear manner. The hearts symbolise love and devotion; the house is a traditional symbol of the gate to the Kingdom of Heaven. The trees represent the Tree of Life.

MATERIALS

1 piece of 14-count Aida fabric

THREADS

1 skein each of the following colours:
  deep rose
  medium rose
  light rose
  light blue
  deep blue
  very deep green
  medium green
  light green
  soft yellow

INSTRUCTIONS

Two strands are used for all cross-stitching, and one strand for all of the backstitching, using a no. 25 tapestry needle.

The finished design measures 7in x 8³⁄₈in (18cm x 31cm) or 99 x 119 squares.

Colour Key

✱	deep rose
✕	medium rose
＼	light rose
ǀ	light blue
＋	deep blue
☐	very deep green
◢	medium green
／	light green
○	soft yellow

Backstitch — 1 thread
All other — 2 threads

To the house of a friend
the way is never long

14. *"Love is a Gift"*

This is a pretty sampler, and one that makes a perfect gift for someone that you love, or for a couple who are to be married.

MATERIALS

1 piece of 14-count Aida 12in (29cm) x 16in (40.5cm)

THREADS

1 skein of deep pink stranded cotton
1 skein of pewter grey stranded cotton

INSTRUCTIONS

Find the centre of the fabric. With two strands of thread, work the design as shown on pages 94, 95.

It would be easier to start with the horizontal pink stitches of the ribbon as this will give you a guide for the rest of the design. You can substitute colours of your choice.

FINISHING

A piece of mounting board 6½in (16.5cm) x 10in (25cm). This can be plain or with adhesive. Mount this according to the earlier instructions. We framed our sampler with a pewter grey aluminium frame for effect.

Colour Key

- pink
✕ grey

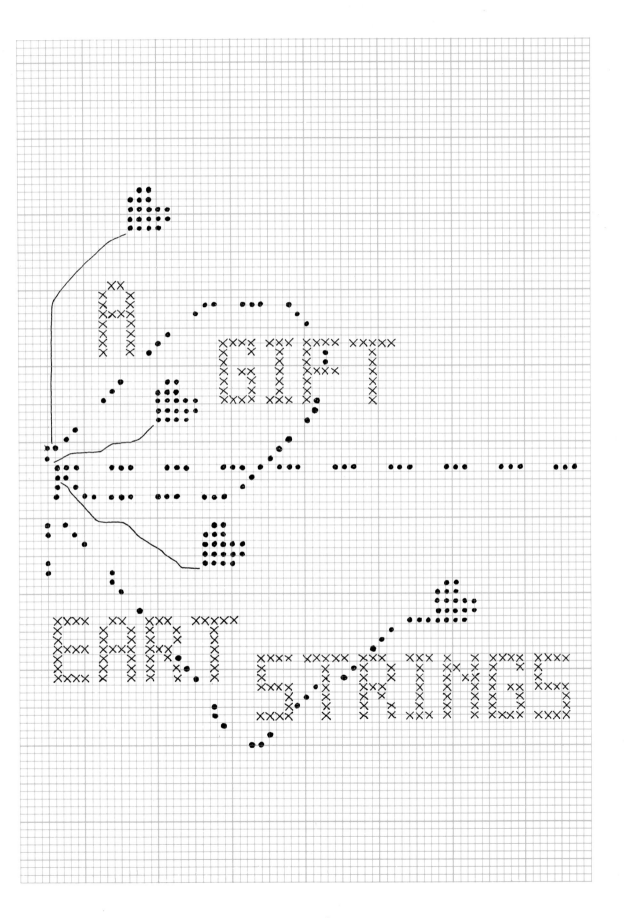

15. Butterfly T-Shirt

Any design can be transferred to a T-shirt or sweat shirt by using waste canvas. Here we have designed a butterfly for you to work.

MATERIALS

1 T-shirt
1 piece of waste canvas 6in (15cm)
   x 6in (15cm) in 10 stitches to the inch

THREADS

1 skein each of stranded cotton in the following colours

   black
   yellow
   red orange
   dark tan
   light tan

INSTRUCTIONS

Place the waste canvas in position on T-shirt and tack around it, and diagonally, to hold it firm. Do not stretch the T-shirt too much as this will distort the design.

This design can be worked from top to bottom using the waste canvas as your guide. Make sure you have enough room to fit the design in on either side. A good idea is to find the centre of the graph and, working from the top, count out to the first stitch. Make sure your needle goes into the hole and does not split the canvas. You will note that the waste canvas is made up of groups of 4 threads. Work over each group as though it was solid, like the Aida cloth.

FINISHING

When you have finished working the design (except the feelers), pull out the tacking threads. CAREFULLY cut away the waste canvas from around the design leaving about ½ in (1.2cm) to 1in (2.4cm) all round. With a pair of tweezers, or by hand, GENTLY pull the strands of canvas out, one by one. If one should be difficult, leave it and go on to the next one. You may find that it will help to release the difficult one.

When this step is finished, use one strand of black thread to stem stitch the feelers on the butterfly.

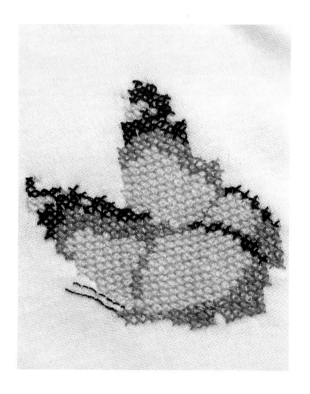

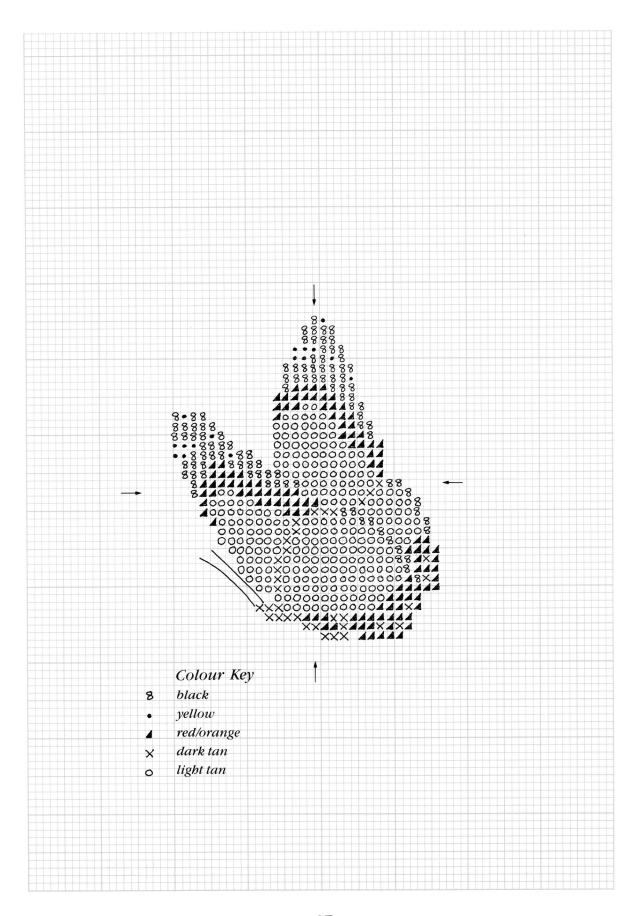

Colour Key

8	*black*
•	*yellow*
◢	*red/orange*
×	*dark tan*
○	*light tan*

16. Grandmother's Treasures

This design shows the grand-children's names and can be adapted for any number. The name could also be MOTHER'S TREASURES. All that is required is to centre the words accordingly. To do this, use a piece of graph paper 10 to the 1in.

An alphabet is shown for you to do the appropriate names. Again, centre the name at the bottom of each flower. The flowers may be done in any colours you like.

MATERIALS

1 piece of 14-count Aida 12in (29cm) x 16in (40.5cm)

THREADS

1 skein of apple green
1 skein of pink
5 colours for the flowers eg: red, yellow (centre of blue flower), orange, pink, blue and purple.

INSTRUCTIONS

Find the centre of fabric and mark it. Mark the centre of the graph and then decide where to start and count the required rows.

FINISHING

A piece of mounting board 6in (15cm) x 9in (25.5cm). This can be plain or with adhesive. Mount this according to the earlier instructions.

Frame used in the illustration is a green aluminium.

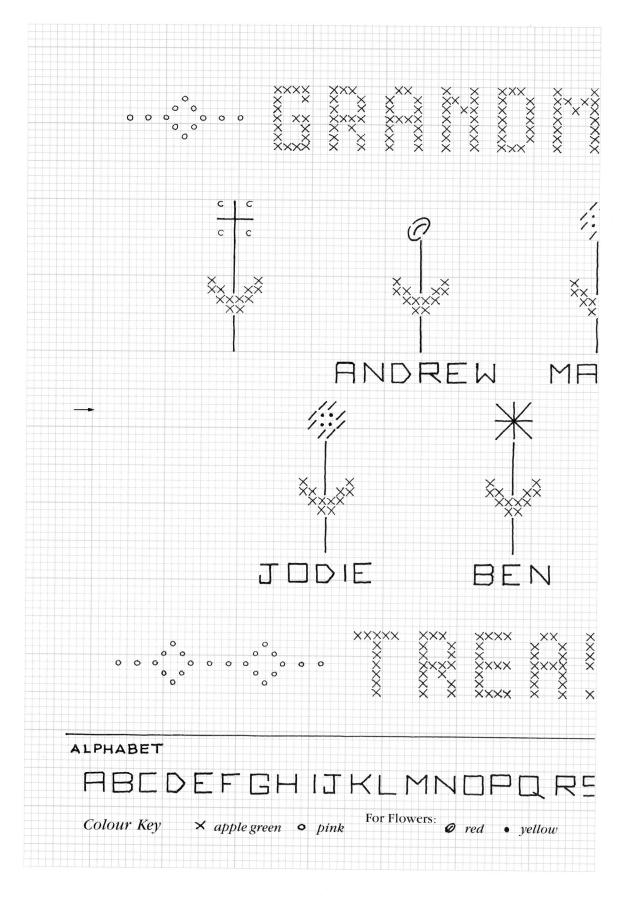

ALPHABET

ABCDEFGHIJKLMNOPQRS

Colour Key ✗ *apple green* ○ *pink* For Flowers: ❂ *red* • *yellow*

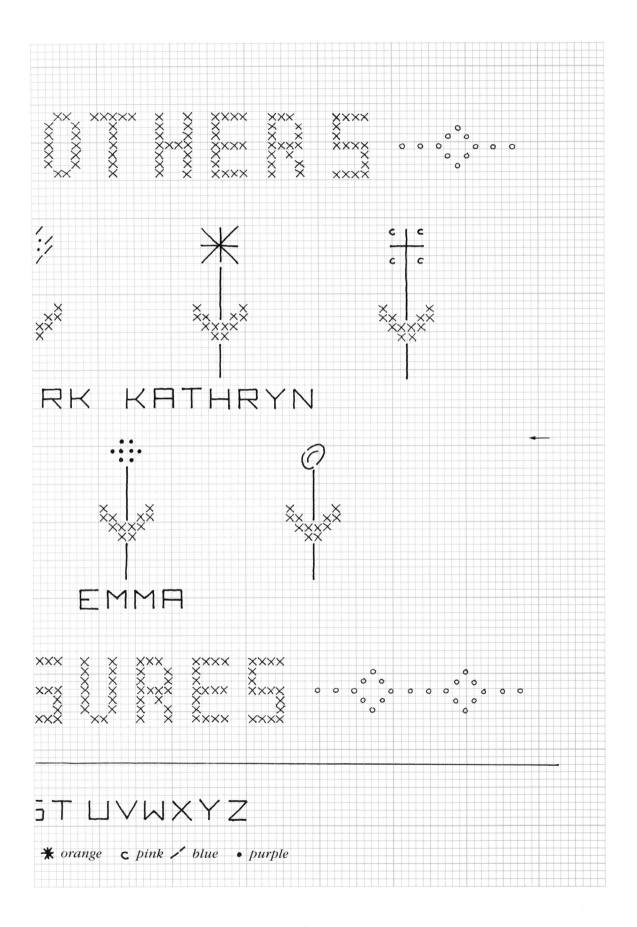

RK KATHRYN

EMMA

GT UVWXYZ

✳ *orange*   c *pink* ∕ *blue* • *purple*

17. Christmas Boot Decoration

MATERIALS

1 10in square of white 14-count Aida
   fabric
1 10in square of backing fabric
1 5in diameter frame
fabric glue
½ yrd (m) of braid

THREADS

1 skein each of stranded cotton in the
following colours:

    dark green
    light green
    dark red coral
    medium red coral
    white
    grey
    pale yellow
    christmas red
    black

INSTRUCTIONS

Centre the design on the fabric and
stitch from the centre. Place Aida
fabric in frame with the centre of the
design in line with the handle. Make
sure all of the woven rows of Aida are
straight. Cut away the excess fabric at
the back of the frame. Glue a circle of
backing fabric on to the back of the
frame to cover the reverse side of the
cross-stitch design. Trim the excess
fabric back to the frame.

Glue the braid around the edge of
the frame at the back to completely
cover the raw edges of the backing
fabric.

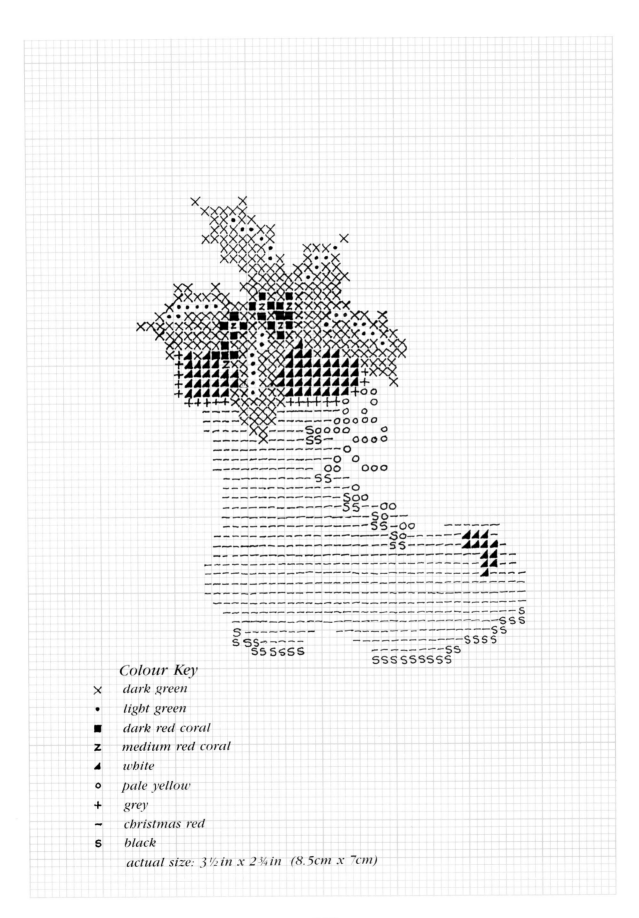

Colour Key

✕	dark green
•	light green
■	dark red coral
z	medium red coral
◢	white
o	pale yellow
+	grey
~	christmas red
s	black

actual size: 3½in x 2¾in (8.5cm x 7cm)

18. Wedding Pillow

The colours can be altered to match the wedding party's colours. This design can be worked in Aida but to get the same size you would have to use 11-count Aida fabric.

To work on Aida, backstitch the circle onto the Aida and then work it in the same way.

The finished pillow measures approximately 9in (23cm) in diameter.

MATERIALS

1 12in (30.5cm) square of Zweigart Constance damask
1 square of satin to back pillow
wadding to fill
lace to edge
1 yard (metre) of white ribbon
1 yard (metre) of tangerine ribbon

THREADS

1 skein of tangerine embroidery cotton
1 skein of old gold embroidery cotton

INSTRUCTIONS

Use two strands of thread. The cross in the middle is done twice to hold the ribbons. Tie the ribbon once. Place rings in through the ribbon and tie in a firm bow.

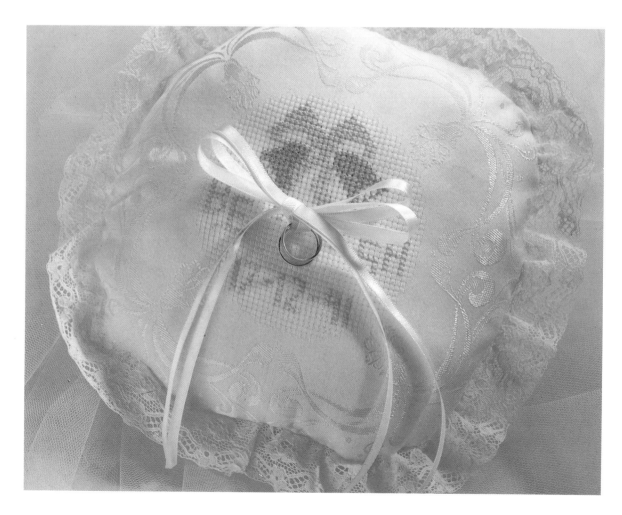

Colour Key

× light tangerine
o old gold

19. Afternoon Tea Cloth

MATERIALS

1 piece of 18in (45.5cm) square white Lugano fabric (25 threads to the inch) or any even-weave fabric of equivalent thread count.

1¼ yd (1.14m) white cotton crochet lace

Tracing paper

Compass

THREADS

1 skein each of the following colours:

dark avocado green

medium olive green

rose pink

medium rose pink

dark rose pink

light rose pink

very light avocado green

light avocado green

INSTRUCTIONS

Make a pattern on the tracing paper of 10½ in (26.5cm) diameter circle.

Place this pattern on the square worked with the rose, with the design centred. Cut out the fabric.

If the lace has no selvedge, use a fancy overlock stitch on the sewing machine to attach the lace and bind the fabric edges at the same time. Place the lace on the fabric, right sides facing and raw edges together. Sew in place. Lift the lace up and fold the fabric seam inwards. Iron well so that the cloth lies flat.

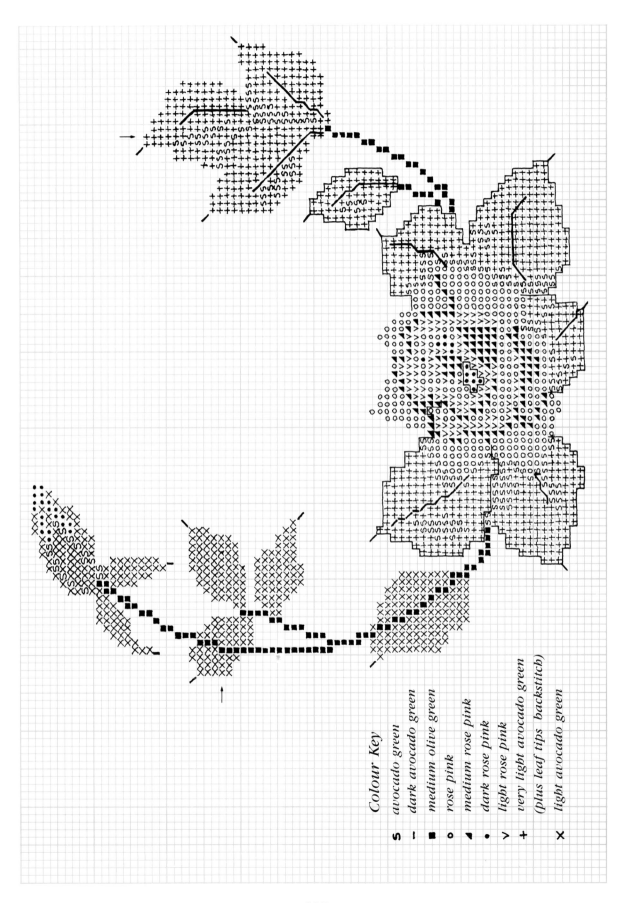

Colour Key

S	avocado green
–	dark avocado green
■	medium olive green
o	rose pink
◣	medium rose pink
•	dark rose pink
>	light rose pink
+	very light avocado green (plus leaf tips backstitch)
X	light avocado green

20. Nasturtium Cushion

MATERIALS

½ yd (.5m) of Country or Rustic
14-count Aida
1 skein of very dark forest green
stranded cotton for the Alphabet
1 15in (38cm) cushion insert
Length of cording to finish cushion
measuring approx. 5ft (1.5m) is
optional.

THREADS

1 skein each of:

    dark forest green
    medium yellow green
    very light avocado green
    ultra light avocado green
    medium olive green
    light olive green
    red copper
    dark burnt orange
    burnt orange
    light pumpkin
    medium tangerine
    deep canary
    light golden wheat

INSTRUCTIONS

Cut the fabric to a square ie:
½ yard by ½ a yard (.5m x .5m)

Find the centre of the graph and
mark the fabric.

It is very important to make sure
that the Alphabet is placed correctly.
Work the Alphabet first, starting at the
centre and working down and
right/left. Complete the other side.
Turn graph around and fabric around

and work the same for the top. You
will actually be working upside down,
but the crosses will still be the same
way.

When you have completed the
Alphabet, it will be easier to work the
flowers as the positioning will be
counted from the respective letters
involved.

FINISHING

When the work is finished, iron it
on the wrong side on a folded towel.
This will raise the design.

From the other piece of the fabric,
cut another square the same size to
back the cushion. You may choose to
use a different kind of fabric for this,
but the instructions will be the same.
Mark the square the size of 15in
(38cm) by using a tacking thread all
round. This should give you a 1½in
(3.7cm) turning on the cushion.
Keeping a straight seam, stitch three
sides of the cushion. Turn it inside out
and press carefully. Press in the seam
allowance on the fourth side to make
it easier to close up. Insert the cushion
padding. Attach the end of the cording
to one of the open corners tucking the
end inside. Carefully catch the cording
along the seam of the cushion to the
other corner. Carefully close the top
by hand and before finishing off, stitch
the rest of the cording tucking the end
in with the other end. Finish off the
corner neatly.

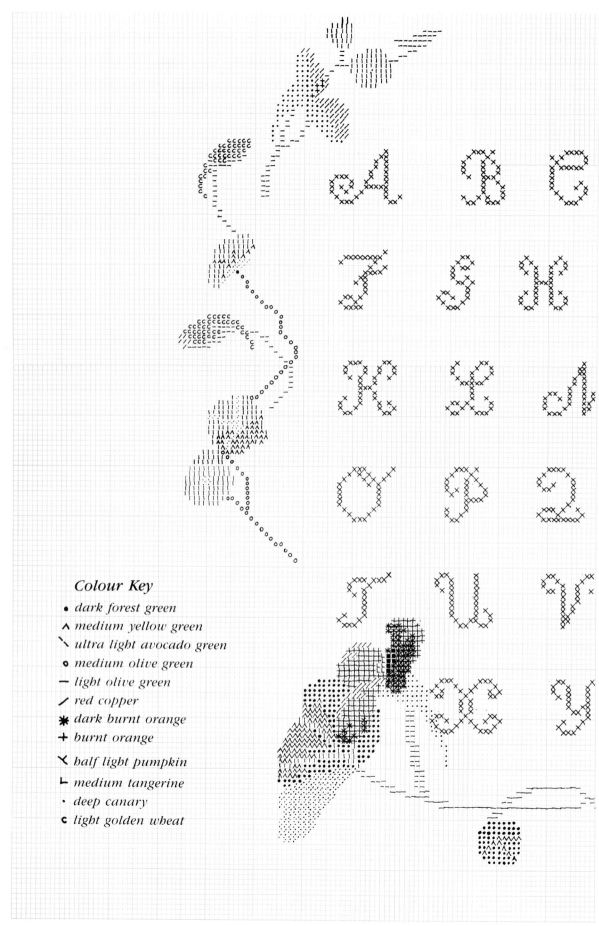

Colour Key

- • dark forest green
- ∧ medium yellow green
- ∖ ultra light avocado green
- ○ medium olive green
- — light olive green
- ∕ red copper
- ✳ dark burnt orange
- + burnt orange
- ✕ half light pumpkin
- ∟ medium tangerine
- · deep canary
- c light golden wheat

Index

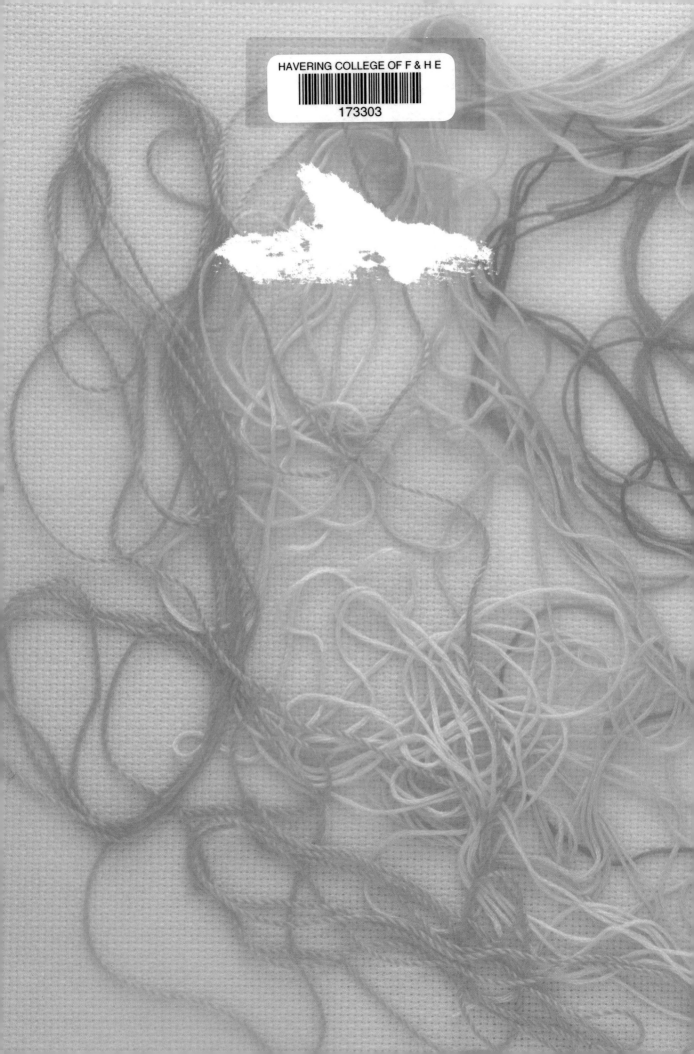